GOD'S
CITY
IN THE
JUNGLE

SANNA BARLOW ROSSI

GOD'S CITY IN THE JUNGLE

WITHDRAWN

WYCLIFFE BIBLE TRANSLATORS, INC.

Huntington Beach, California 92648

Cover photo: Ed Riggle
of Wycliffe Bible Translators
working with the Cashibo tribe
in Shambayu, Peru.
(John Chao)

Library of Congress
Catalog Card Number
74-21968
ISBN 8423-1070-3
Copyright © 1975
Tyndale House Publishers, Inc.,
Wheaton, Illinois.
All rights reserved.
First printing:
January 1975. Printed in the
United States of America

Contents

List of Photographs

Foreword

BILLY GRAHAM

Someone once said, "A balanced reading diet is necessary for healthy spiritual growth." The Christian, along with his other reading, would do well to continually be reading and meditating in at least three books: the Bible, the hymnal, and a Christian biography.

God's City in the Jungle is a twentieth-century missionary story that unfolds the evident blessing of God on the lives of a choice Wycliffe Translator couple, Lambert and Doris Anderson. You will share in their call to the mission field and their subsequent training. It is exciting to see them discover and develop their peculiar gifts as members of the Body of Christ. It is evident that Lambert and Doris found maximum joy during the twenty-one years they spent in Peru, ministering to the Ticuna Indian tribe clustered around a beautiful lake deep in the jungle.

The work of translators of the Bible calls for the most daring and trusting spirits, the keenest and most disciplined minds, linked with the selfless and patient love for those who need to hear of new life in Christ.

It is my prayer that through this book many young people and adults will be stirred to become the uniquely gifted persons that God intended for them to be. As you read, perhaps God will call you to find your way to that exceptional group of translators and support team known as "The Wycliffe Bible Translators."

Preface

SANNA BARLOW ROSSI

If you were to fly by airliner to Peru, South America, and then charter a helicopter to the northeast corner, you would see the thick jungle opening up to reveal an Indian village on a beautiful lake just off the Amazon River. The story of this village and its people—amazingly transformed in the past twenty years—becomes the true drama of this book. Lambert and Doris Anderson, following the leading of God, found in this village a treasure—a community of neglected people who recovered the noble heritage of true manhood through the leadership and teaching of the Andersons. Today God speaks to the Ticunas in their own language through the Scriptures translated by these Wycliffe Bible Translators, and the Ticunas' response has brought a renaissance to these descendants of the Incas.

The Ticunas are one of over five hundred tribal groups served by Wycliffe in some two dozen countries. Though three thousand members make up Wycliffe's translation force—including doctors, pilots, nurses, teachers, mechanics, printers, electricians, builders, typists, and office workers—hundreds of tribes still await an opportunity to hear God speak in their language. And unconsciously—they await the wondrous changes celebrated by the heaven-touched Ticunas.

Chapter One **BEACHHEAD**

The rough-hewn dugout canoe dipped and rose gently in the current of the brown-running Amazon. Cargo filled the narrow, twenty-foot craft except for spaces in the middle and stern that were occupied by two men. One was blond and raw boned, and obviously a bit uneasy about the trackless waterway and the thick jungle crowding the shorelines. The second man, lean and tanned, guided the tiller of a throbbing outboard motor. He scanned the shores expectantly and smiled encouragement to his quizzical companion.

"How much farther?" called the blond-thatched passenger.

"My guess is as bad as yours!" responded his partner wryly. "It's fifteen hundred miles to the Atlantic Ocean, but only about a hundred to the Peru-Brazil border."

Perhaps another half-day, then, to the Indian settlement in the northeastern corner of Peru. Lambert Anderson, the transplanted gringo, shifted to a more comfortable position and leaned back to reflect on his future waiting somewhere ahead on the mighty Amazon River.

It was hard to realize he might be close to his new home for the next decade or so. From Wisconsin, U.S.A., to Amazonia, Peru. And from raising cattle and grain to learning the unwritten language of an obscure Indian tribe, the Ticunas. What did the Ticunas really mean to Lambert —and to his effervescent wife Doris who awaited the results of this exploratory trip?

The Ticunas meant some danger, as they were reputed to be excitable people with serious problems of drunkenness and suicide, and were famed for their poisoned blowguns. But the tribe had regular contacts with traders from the outside world, and their poison arrows killed only animals, supposedly. Lambert had no strong apprehensions about his safety.

Adventure and challenge also lay ahead. Only a year and half out of college, Lambert and Doris faced the formidable task of lifting the Ticunas into modern civilization through education. Until the Ticunas could read and write, they were doomed to poverty, subservience, and ignorance. Their first step to freedom would be the ability to read their own language—which had not yet been written! But that was the Andersons' specialty: analyzing a spoken language and constructing its written form so new readers could plunge into the wide world of knowledge.

Lambert felt sure of some other rewards: if Ticunaland became his home, there would be less drunkenness among the Indians and more community development; there would be less family strife and more sharing of goals; there would even be radically changed individuals because the Andersons planned to translate the Bible into Ticuna and introduce the Indians to the living God through his written revelations.

The prospect sent a shiver down Lambert's spine, just as it had that blustery November day in Wisconsin when the letter from Cameron Townsend, director of Wycliffe Bible Translators, urged them to head immediately for Peru —they needed another couple to write God's message in a new language. And now the Andersons were ready to begin—pioneers . . . builders . . . harvesters of people for God—nothing else in the world seemed more exciting to Lambert.

"Look over there."

The words startled Lambert. He quickly looked back at his companion, Wes Thiesen, and then followed the line of his pointing finger. A tiny cluster of houses on stilts, half-hidden among the trees on the river bank, seemed to beckon the travelers. Wes angled the boat toward the settlement, and in no time they were wading in the water, pulling the canoe's prow onto the bank. The boat secure, they headed toward the first hut and immediately spotted an alert-looking man with black hair and dark-bronze skin. Lambert's attention was drawn to his pointed teeth; could they mean he was a Ticuna?

"Do you speak Ticuna?" Wes inquired in Spanish.

"Yes," he replied. "I myself am a Ticuna."

The visitors were delighted to be invited into the thatched-roof house. The floors were split-palm and the room was without walls. A fire-table was built on one side, and little clay jugs were scattered on the floor. A blowgun hung up under the rafters. And watching the visitors curiously were bright-eyed children. Their eyes widened when the blond guest began using his limited Spanish to ask the Ticuna words.

"How do you say 'hand'?"

"Naxmex."

With notebook in hand Lambert wrote down every reply.

"How do you say 'foot'? 'Head'? What is the word for 'brother,' 'father,' 'sister,' 'house,' 'canoe,' 'paddle,' 'machete'?" Two hours of questioning filled several pages of the notebook with the rare treasure of Lambert's first Ticuna words.

Sometimes the words were quite easy to hear and write in phonetical script. Other sounds were more subtle, and Wes, borrowing on his translating experience with the Bora Indians, helped Lambert decipher the differences. It was an exhilarating start, but Lambert's assignment was to appraise the entire tribal situation and look for a suitable site to build his own leaf-thatch house!

Assured that more Ticunas were downriver, Wes and Lambert thanked their hosts and resumed their journey. They passed cluster after cluster of homes, and then people at every settlement affirmed: "Yes, yes, we are Ticunas!" Each encounter added to Lambert's prized list.

At four o'clock they came to Caballococha, the last Peruvian town of any size before the Brazilian border. It was a river town with about fifteen hundred people and a hospital, police post, school, and other government units. At the rustic police post, Lambert and Wes checked in to present their official documents and explained their river mission.

After the preliminaries, Wes said, "We've heard of a lake called Cushillococha; would it be possible for us to visit the Ticunas living there?"

The police chief shook his head. "No," he demurred. "That's a dangerous place. You'd have to take policemen with you. The Ticunas there are bad about drinking and brawling."

The men looked at each other. The presence of policemen on the first visit of a friendly mission would give the wrong impression. Carefully the Bible translators explained their situation to the official, and he finally gave permission for them to explore Cushillococha alone.

It was six o'clock when Lambert and Wes left Caballococha. When darkness fell they were approaching an abandoned hut standing on stilts above the flood waters which the owner had evidently left because of the rising river. As the floor was still above the water level, the travelers decided to dock there for the night. They hitched their canoe to a corner post and moved their sleeping gear inside. Lulled by the croaks of frogs, the flutter and screeches of night birds, and the deep roar of howler monkeys in the distance, the invaders drifted into a sound sleep.

As a new dawn mirrored gloriously over the flood waters, Lambert and Wes ate a quick breakfast and pushed on their way again. They shook their heads as they passed mile after mile of Ticuna homes standing in the water, in some cases up to the roofs. An hour of travel and several inquiries brought them to a narrow channel leading off to the right. This was the stream they had been looking for, the waterway to the Ticuna lake. It was enchantingly beautiful, winding into the deep jungle where varied species of rainforest trees intermingled with towering palms, and tropical birds chorused their progress. Frequently it was necessary to stop the dugout and chop through logs before they could proceed.

An hour and a half of jungle wonderland had dropped behind when suddenly the most picturesque lake they could imagine stretched before them: it was about four miles long and one-half mile wide—Cushillococha.

Slowly they entered the lake and moved across the gently rippling water. About one-third of the way along its length, they spotted the first of the twenty-five houses reaching down the shore. Stopping at the first house, they talked with the residents and Lambert noted words for future use. They went from house to house, introducing themselves and groping for Ticuna words.

By two o'clock they were near the center of the settlement, chatting with a Ticuna named Pablo. As they visited, a canoe drew near, its Indian occupant paddling rapidly and shouting excitedly.

"What's happened?" Wes asked in Spanish. Pablo interpreted in the Spanish he knew: "The chief of the village has just been bitten by a shushupi snake!"

Wes knew this was a bushmaster, one of the most poisonous of the jungle snakes. The visitors jumped into their canoe and kicked the motor into high for a fast trip back to the first house they had visited coming into Cushillococha.

There they found Chief Cuaachitu writhing in pain near the edge of the floor while family and friends watched in fear from the other side of the room. Someone had tied a vine around his arm, but the deadly venom was already coursing into the victim's bloodstream.

Wes leaped into the house, a snake bite kit in his hand. He sliced open the wound, making short slashes around the bite. Then he applied the suction device, pulling some of the poison out of the tortured flesh.

"Too dark to make it to Caballococha tonight," Wes muttered. "Even by the shortcuts the Ticunas know, we can't do it."

"But we could take off at dawn," Lambert blurted. "I'm sure the doctor there can help him."

"We'll leave at first light," Wes agreed, and he explained their plans to Pablo and the huddled family.

The next morning they roared over a short-cut through the flooded jungle and made it quickly to the hospital in Caballococha. "Fortunately, I have anti-venom on hand!" the doctor greeted them. He commended Wes and Lambert for their first-aid treatment as he gave the life-giving injection to the chief. In a short time the chief was on the way to a remarkable recovery.

"If you had not been here, this man would have died," the Indians later told their visitors in the village. To Lambert, it seemed a clear sign that God wanted to minister to the Ticunas through him.

Five more days were spent in the midst of the Ticunas in a cordial atmosphere. New words filtered through interpretive pens into the missionaries' notebooks. They found that a few Indian men could communicate in limited Spanish, but among themselves they used their own language exclusively.

Deciding to explore the tribal territory farther downstream, Lambert and Wes checked on their *Salvo Conducto* permit and set out for the Colombia border city of Leticia. From there they traveled into Brazil and found a Ticuna settlement called Mariwazu below the jungle town of Tabatinga. Checking out the language as they went along, they found that it was much the same as that of Cushillococha.

In Tabatinga they came across a book written by a man who had tried to write down the Ticuna language several years before. But there was something so difficult about the phonology of the language that he had decided the Indians must speak different dialects on every stream. "In fact," he concluded peevishly, "they don't even remember their own language from night to morning." It seemed he had jotted down words one day and tried to pronounce them the next day with no sign of recognition from the Indians. Evidently this was no simple language.

Back again in Cushillococha, Lambert tried to imagine his own home with Doris and tiny Betsy here among the Ticunas. He talked to the Indians in Spanish about coming to live in their village. He told them he wanted to learn their language and be their friend. They were instantly agreeable to the plan.

With axes and machetes in hand the following morning, almost all the Indian men around the lake and many of the women and children arrived to help clear a piece of high land along the lake shore near Pablo's house. Lambert chose the site because of its invulnerability to flood water and the presence of three beautiful aguaje palm trees fronting the lake. By noon a large swath of jungle had been chopped down and the house area had been staked out.

Pausing to survey their progress, Lambert realized he had made a major commitment: Cushillococha was to be their home for an indefinite period of toil and service. Though it was six hundred miles from Wycliffe's forward jungle base at Yarinacocha, float planes could land on the lake and boat transport would connect them with the outside world for supplies. It was also relatively near government facilities in Caballococha. Most important, the friendly Ticunas would pour their language into Lambert's ears and notebook, and Spanish-speaking Ticunas would help him learn their puzzling speech.

Christobal Moreno—unknown to Lambert, a local witchdoctor—seemed to be one of the leaders among the workers clearing the house site. Since Lambert had to return to Yarinacocha, he asked Christobal to take charge of constructing an Indian-style house, and Lambert gave him money to pay for labor and materials. Others offered to help bring poles for the framework and leaves to make the roof so it would be ready when Lambert returned.

Anxious to get back and report on the success of their survey, Lambert and Wes left the beautiful lake for their upstream journey. At San Pablo, a leper colony, they tried to radio a report to the base at Yarinacocha, but they got no response. Later they were to learn that their brief message got through, but a defect in the receiver prevented an acknowledgement.

Two days afterward, the weary travelers passed the town of Pebas and entered the Ampiyaco River for an hour's trip to Estiron where another Wycliffe team, the Eugene Minors, worked on the Witoto tribal language. Here they knew a functioning radio existed, kept in operation by the Wycliffe auxiliary agency, Jungle Aviation and Radio Service. Their first thought was to call Yarinacocha.

But before they could call they heard the roar of a JAARS Aeronca. In minutes it had landed on the river and the pilot soon brought them the word that their radio message from San Pablo had gotten through. Relieved and grateful, Lambert looked forward to the morning flight back to Iquitos, Peru's jungle capital, and the remaining four-hour hop south to Yarinacocha—and to Doris.

What would she say about his discovery—and his decision to build their jungle home? As Lambert wondered, it seemed that beautiful Cushillococha could almost be a dream and he, a college-trained farm boy, was still in peaceful Wisconsin. Had his short life prepared him for the physical and spiritual rigors springing from jungle soil?

Native sugar cane press fashioned from hand-hewn "bloodwood," one of the hardest and most beautiful of the jungle woods. (Don Hesse)

Chapter Two **CHOSEN!**

Lambert was the only son of Emil and Lillian Anderson, and his father expected that some day Lambert would take over the dairy farm outside Oconto Falls in northeast Wisconsin. But as a teen-ager driving the tractor long hours under the clear blue skies, Lambert began to listen for God's direction, and he thought he heard a call to serve God in a special way—in another country.

The local Youth for Christ club was a factor in Lambert's questing, and so were the musical groups from St. Paul Bible College in St. Paul, Minnesota, that occasionally visited Lambert's church in Oconto. One night while reading the New Testament in his room, Lambert turned over his life to God and pledged to do whatever God planned for him. As high school days dropped behind, attending a Bible college for Christian training seemed to be part of God's plan.

The issue settled, Lambert enrolled in St. Paul Bible College for two years after high school. In his sophomore year he met a tall, dark-haired, and full-of-life girl, Doris Geist. She came to St. Paul from Warrendale, Pennsylvania, after Nyack Missionary College in New York —where her three older sisters attended—asked the seventeen-year-old Doris to wait another year before enrolling. A music enthusiast, Doris had already studied piano at the Pittsburgh Musical Institute, and she decided not to defer college another year. Though her music lessons took hours a day just to play through assigned pieces, she found time to date the farm boy from Wisconsin. Sometimes the "dates" were missionary meetings listening to speakers tell of the needs in foreign countries. They frequently read the Bible together, and as school days slipped by, Doris considered the possibility that the Lord might want her in missionary work. She thought of the possibility of teaching music to missionary children.

An assignment in English composition led Lambert to research the Inca empire, and he became fascinated by the marvelous attainments of the fifteenth-century kingdom in South America. Returning from the library one afternoon, Lambert stopped at the room of his friend Roy David, also from Wisconsin. Roy was out, but his roommate Waldo Pust, was there, and Lambert's exuberance overflowed.

"Waldo, I'm working on a paper about the ancient Incas of Peru—and they were fabulous!"

"You know, I plan to go to Peru some day," Waldo replied seriously. "They need pilots in the jungles there. I have my license, and I've already applied to the Wycliffe Bible Translators. I hope to join the Jungle Aviation and Radio Service."

Suddenly Lambert was confronted with the reality of contemporary Indian tribes in Peru. It was his introduction to the Wycliffe Bible Translators—an acquaintance that was to grow in interest and commitment. He quickly caught the inspiration of the mission from its namesake, John Wycliffe, the Britisher who first translated the whole Bible in English.

Miracle was bursting from the trees and shining in the fresh grasses and flowers around St. Paul in April 1950. Twenty-two-year-old Lambert Anderson realized summer vacation was near and he had not yet shared with Doris the thoughts of his heart about the future. One evening toward the end of the month he told her he knew the Lord was directing him to go to Peru and work with the Wycliffe Bible Translators—did she want to go with him?

She must have been prepared for the big question, but she was not yet ready for a full answer. That summer

Lambert visited her family in Pennsylvania and during a happy stay she accepted his proposal of marriage—and missionary career. They spent the following year in college with Doris shifting her major to Christian education in preparation for teaching in a foreign land.

May 29 was Lambert's graduation day, and four days afterward he and Doris were married. Their honeymoon was a fast trip to the University of Oklahoma in Norman where they enrolled in the Summer Institute of Linguistics —their first step toward joining the Wycliffe team.

At S.I.L. a new scope of knowledge rushed into view—a new vocabulary. They heard the words *phonetics*, *phonemics*, *semantics*, *morphology*, and other terms that gradually came alive. Despite the 100 degree temperatures of summertime Norman, the Andersons got excited over the challenge of unraveling a language and putting it together in meaningful patterns. But their initial delight was far from an assurance that they could put the Bible in an unwritten language!

"To you is this word of salvation sent"—the words reverberated from Acts 13:26 and pierced the hearts of the Wycliffe trainees. That was the sublime purpose and prospect of Bible translators dedicated to reaching the "you" in every tribe with God's truth.

Students analyzing some of the languages of U.S. Indians—Kiowa, Comanche, Cheyenne, and Arapaho— were amazed at orderly patterns of grammar. In phonetics they studied all the sounds from the known languages of the world. They learned about the phenomenon of a tonal language in which syllables of a single word are spoken with varying pitches to give different meanings.

"Tonal languages are rare," said their instructor. "Usually only two or three levels of pitch are involved." It was noted that Bob Longacre in Mexico had discovered five levels of tone in the Trique language, something almost unheard of. Tone drills were fun for Doris because of her sensitive ear for music, but her husband joked: "The two of us make 100 percent on the tone drills—if we add my 2 percent to Doris's 98."

The Andersons heard much about the man who had founded Wycliffe seventeen years earlier and who had begun the first Summer Institute of Linguistics with three students in 1934. He was ex-missionary William Cameron Townsend, or "Uncle Cam" as he is affectionately known to old and young, politicians and peasants.

"Lambert," exclaimed Doris one evening, "we're invited to dinner at the Townsends tomorrow!" With other students they had the joy of getting acquainted with Uncle Cam and his charming wife Elaine the following evening. For a mission leader, Uncle Cam was unexpectedly mild mannered, but his geniality and sincere interest in everyone appealed strongly to the Andersons. The new friendship confirmed their inclination to seek membership in the mission.

Uncle Cam remembered the Andersons later when their names came up at an official meeting considering candidates for appointment to tribal translation work. Someone suggested that Doris, only nineteen years old, might be too young for acceptance, and Uncle Cam countered with a twinkle in his eye: "Don't worry about her—that's the age we like to get them and then we can bring them up the way they should go!"

Before the eleven-week session closed in August, the approved candidates were notified of their acceptance as members of Wycliffe and the Summer Institute of Linguistics: Lambert and Doris were included, and they became numbers 492 and 493 on the mission's lengthening list of "revolutionaries through literature."

Chapter Three **LAUNCHED**

Through Mexico's mountains Doris and Lambert coaxed their twelve-year-old Ford, nicknamed Susie. They were headed for Wycliffe's Jungle Camp, after a pause in Mexico City. The required training in jungle pioneering tested all of Wycliffe's young appointees. The Andersons talked about their new adventure as they approached Mexico City. "How does one build a hut out of raw jungle?" Lambert speculated.

It was evening as they descended a precipitous highway into Mexico City and Susie's lights began to flick off and on temperamentally as they rounded steep curves. Fortunately, they could see the tail lights of fellow recruit George Insley's car just ahead, and by keeping close, Lambert managed to stay on the road. After some tense maneuvering they leveled out and found their way to Wycliffe's hub of operations in Mexico, "The Kettle."

Everything was mobilized for action in the one large building—offices for shipping and finance, printing facilities, dining room, and living quarters for couples and families. The Kettle maintained contact with all the linguists in sixty tribes throughout Mexico, and the place was full to the brim. Lambert and Doris quickly caught the excitement permeating the Mexican nerve center.

After two days the Andersons were on their way again toward Jungle Camp in Mexico's southern peninsula. Susie trundled them through Oaxaca and on to Ixtapa in the state of Chiapas where E. W. Hatcher of Missionary Aviation Fellowship was waiting for them. "Hatch" loaded them into his little plane, piled in their duffels, sleeping bags, and supplies, and then flew them another hundred miles to Jungle Base. The camp turned out to be a cluster of forty palm-thatch huts at the edge of the Yasha-quintala River in Tzeltal tribal country, about fifty miles from the Guatemala border.

Lambert and Doris launched into primitive living as a purposeful lark. Each day was filled with surprises —learning to steer dugout canoes through rapids, endurance swimiing, and overnight survival hikes. One trek ended at a settlement of the Lacandone Indians where translators Phil and Mary Baer were working. Night enveloped them on the trail, and they retired in hammocks hung under the trees. Rain on the hammock roof meant they would plow through mud the next day.

The biggest challenge was a twenty-mile hike to Advance Base—on the other side of a mountain. Climbing and descending, penetrating dense jungle, and fording streams were the order of the day. They arrived late in the afternoon only to find the pack mules with some of the sleeping gear were unaccounted for. Lambert and several others doubled back in search of the recalcitrant animals. At dusk they located the mule drivers and learned two of the pack animals were lost. An hour's effort rounded up the quarry, and two hours later the stragglers trudged into camp. They gave only passing notice to food before collapsing into tree-swung hammocks for the night.

But Lambert's day wasn't over. Something terribly annoying soon awoke him. Tiny creatures were scurrying all over him and he was desperate to find out what they were. Doris came with a flashlight that disclosed a multitude of wood ticks evidently picked up on the trail. Two sets of flashlight batteries wore out as Doris picked off four hundred twenty-seven rampaging ticks! At last sleep came and assuaged Lambert's aches.

Jungle Camp meant new friendships that would last through the years. Among them were numbered future pilot Ralph Borthwick and his wife, and Lee Duncan (later Lee Kindberg, who with her husband Will would complete the translation of the New Testament for Peru's Campa Indians). Don Van Wynen directed activities at Advance Base and taught the young recruits how to literally carve out a liveable settlement in the jungle.

At night everyone gathered around a campfire to sing God's praise and share spiritual lessons being learned. Personal Bible study, a regular part of the day's schedule, deepened devotional life and fed the motive of their endeavor. The character and conduct of the missionaries were to be very important as they taught Christian truths through words.

Doris and Lambert left Jungle Camp some pounds lighter but with new fiber and confidence in their souls. They returned to Mexico City and found The Kettle bubbling with activity. Bob Longacre had just arrived and he asked Doris to help him by writing down musical notes as Bob's Indian informant sang Trique hymns. It wasn't difficult to get the notes of the melody written down except for one problem—"They sing between the notes!" Doris exclaimed. "For instance, they sing between F and F#. I'm continually having to write in accidentals where the Triques insist on singing in the cracks!" But the experience was another educational leap ahead.

Lambert and Doris returned to Norman, Oklahoma, in the summer of 1952 for advanced studies at the Summer Institute of Linguistics. They tackled a specific Indian language—Kiowa for Lambert and Cheyenne for Doris—to stretch their understanding of their main task ahead. It was an exhilarating summer for the husband-wife team, and graduation brought an official letter notifying them they had been assigned to the country of their choice—Peru!

Elated, the Andersons traveled to Wisconsin and Pennsylvania to tell mission-hearted churches of their acceptance. The news provoked enthusiasm and promises of prayer, but no offers of financial support. They waited, and weeks crawled by. It was so difficult to remain in their homeland when their hearts had already vaulted to Peru, but they waited God's timing.

In October Uncle Cam wrote: "When are you coming?" and asked an immediate answer.

"We're ready any time, but support has not materialized—nothing yet."

Back came Uncle Cam's reply, "Lambert, we really need you both down here right away. The Lord has proved to me over the years that he can take care of our needs no matter what they are. I believe that you should come right down here and let's trust the Lord together to take care of your needs." Doris and Lambert thought of the Scripture, "Casting all your care upon him for he careth for you." It was time to go! As they got things together to travel, Lambert's father made six crates for packing and equipped them with hinges and locks so that they would be usable as cupboards in their future tribal home. Last-minute gifts paid for their plane tickets, and final farewells came on November 19, 1952, when Lambert's family drove them three hundred miles to the Chicago airport. Changing planes in Miami, they flew into a spectacular sunset and south toward the unknown. Looking out at the broad wing of the plane, they were buoyed with the new faith—"On his wings your course is one/with him into cloud or sun/go singing in his ways."

It was after midnight when they dropped into the spread-out lights of Lima, "City of Kings." The capital city on the Pacific coast and home of one and a half million Peruvians was a welcome sight. The air was warm and balmy: it was summer below the equator.

Missionaries George Insley and Les Bancroft met the Andersons and took them to the group house of the Summer Institute of Linguistics between the old and new parts of the city. There was always room for more young linguists, and Doris and Lambert took over a one-time pantry reserved especially for them! They were delighted to find that Uncle Cam and "Aunt" Elaine were also at the group house for business matters.

Lima proved an exotic city. Wide boulevards with trees and flowers ran through beautiful urban areas of modern as well as old Spanish architecture. The commerce center downtown had narrow streets and throngs of people. Overhanging balconies reminded the romantic of bygone days when Spanish lovers serenaded peering maidens. Vintage cars jammed in people bound for outlying areas, and street vendors seemed to be everywhere.

The office number "Padre Jeronimo 492" was instantly recognized as the address used by the Andersons for letters from the United States. It was an old building with a huge door to the street and the office bordering a small inner patio. Here Bob Schneider and his staff took care of government relations and a small "buyer's office" in the back processed supplies for the translators over the central highway to the jungle base of Yarinacocha. Ten days in Lima included official inscription at the office of Foreign Relations, and then the Andersons were ready to fly over the snow-capped Andes to Wycliffe's jungle base.

The DC-3 plane landed on a dirt strip at the frontier town of Pucallpa on the Ucayali River, only six miles from Yarinacocha. The operations center was a beautiful settlement of homes on a hook-shaped lake where float planes could land and take off to supply the translators in the tribes. Its houses were built by the linguists to serve as home and study headquarters for six months of each year. Doris and Lambert were given Uncle Cam's home until their own house could be built.

Lambert promptly undertook the project by buying locally sawed lumber and going to work. The house was built in the style of a typical northwoods cottage except that it had single-board walls and rested on five-foot posts. Set among graceful palm trees, the twenty-four by thirty-foot house had walls and floor of cedar boards and corrugated aluminum roof. Lambert hoped to finish before March

—the date of the couple's first Blessed Event!

Lambert built beds and kitchen shelves of leftover cedar boards. Bookcases, a work desk, dining table, and chairs were purchased. By March 15 the Andersons moved in to their completed house and two weeks later, on March 31, baby Betsy arrived. She was named Lillian Elizabeth for her two grandmothers, but everyone seemed to think the blond infant resembled her father.

Two tribes were being considered by Wycliffe leaders for entrance. One was the Sequoia, a tribe in northern Peru close to Ecuador which had already been surveyed. The language was suspected to be tonal, and Lambert wasn't eager for such a monumental conquest!

Ticuna, the other tribe, was a comparatively large group with fifteen hundred Indians in the northeast corner of Peru plus many others across the borders of Colombia and Brazil. The tribal choice was left to the Andersons—and God's guidance. One of the facts Lambert discovered about the Ticunas in researching Yarinacocha's linguistic and anthropological library was that a priest traveled down the Amazon in 1620 and made the first recorded mention of this tribe. What a fearfully long time to remain isolated from the world—and from God!

His study and prayer led Lambert to search out Ticuna-land with Wes Thiesen in mid-April—then to clear a site for their jungle home on the Amazon after the Indians' hearty welcome. Oconto Falls seemed three million miles away!

The Andersons' home overlooking Lake Cushillococha and surrounded by Ticuna homes. (Lambert Anderson)

Chapter Four **HOME**

Lambert needn't have worried about Doris's reaction to his decision to settle at Cushillococha. She was as eager as he—though the move would be complicated slightly by care of an infant daughter. As Lambert planned and prepared for a return trip, he felt a deepening appreciation for the impressive teamwork he saw at Yarinacocha.

Uncle Cam had insisted on this central base from which to reach outward to the tribes. Lake Yarina was perfect for pontoon and amphibian planes flying translators in and out. The communications center maintained daily contact with tribal workers, and technicians kept radios and electronic equipment in good repair. Offices, a medical clinic, a printshop, and an excellent school for missionary children cared for various needs, and here tribal workers could consult each other about language puzzles.

When Lambert showed his Ticuna word lists to experienced linguists, they advised that certain words were problematic, such as those for "grass" and "wasp." Lambert had written them with identical syllables since they sounded the same, though the Indians insisted the words were different. Were they comparable to the English "to," "too," and "two" or had something been overlooked —perhaps a matter of accent?

Cushillococha became a magic word to Lambert and Doris—an adventure fashioned by God for the Andersons and for the Ticunas who had no inkling that God spoke their language.

Getting back to the tribe meant receiving their shipment

from the United States and repacking the boxes for relaying to the jungle. It also involved the shipment of food; staples such as flour, sugar, milk—evaporated and powdered —were trucked from Lima over the Andean highway to Pucallpa, then to the store in Yarinacocha. From there it was shipped north by river boat to Iquitos and then trans-shipped to the outpost at Caballococha.

In early July Lambert said goodbye to Doris and Betsy and flew by JAARS plane all the way to the Indian village. It was a dramatic moment when the plane skimmed onto the lake for the first time, but the excitement was shortlived because the pilot had to take off immediately to reach Iquitos that afternoon. Lambert felt very alone as he watched the plane vanish over the jungle trees. He couldn't even communicate with Yarinacocha because the heavy generator for his radio set was coming later by boat. But he knew his unseen companion was here. And it was time to start work!

He looked around to see how the house was coming. The posts were up and the framework had been tied together to support a part of the leaf-thatch roof. No floors. No walls. Logs and brush were lying around—evidently the project had interfered with drinking parties, but not for long.

Whenever a Ticuna had a lot of work, Lambert learned, normal procedure was to first cook up a big clay pot of yucca, a starch root, and allow it to ferment into an intoxicating beverage. Relatives and friends were then invited to join the toil and pleasure. Some got violently drunk, often with serious consequences.

The next morning Lambert set about to build the floor of the house. This would have to be made from hand-hewn boards brought from the forest by the Indians. He bought them one by one as they were brought by enterprising individuals. Each board had bark edges which had to be sawed straight to make a comparatively tight floor, twenty feet square. By coaxing and encouraging the Indians to continue with the hard work of hewing boards, Lambert was able to get the materials he needed. In the process he learned new Ticuna words.

Two weeks raced by—Doris and Betsy were due in three more days. The split-palm bark walls were going up around the house, and Lambert was sure they would be finished in time. It was afternoon when a message came that the boat shipment had arrived in Caballococha. This meant that the arrival of the generator would enable him to call Yarinacocha before Doris left. Leaving the construction in the hands of the Ticunas, Lambert and a companion started on the jungle trail for Caballococha.

Upon arrival, Lambert located the cargo but he could not secure transport for it until after eight o'clock. It was risky traveling in the dark because of submerged logs and debris in the river, but since time was short Lambert decided to set out with his possessions in a rented canoe powered by a two-horse outboard motor. Down the moon-streaked Amazon, then through the pitch-dark channel, and finally onto Lake Cushillococha proceeded the lone craft, but without mishap. They reached home in a drizzling rain at 4 A.M. A gray dawn approached as they finished hauling boxes up the muddy bank to shelter from the rain.

By seven that morning, Lambert had the generator going and he placed his first call to Yarinacocha. It seemed almost unbelieveable to hear the radio operator six hundred miles away. "Everything's fine here!" Lambert assured the base. "Are Doris and Betsy okay? I'm expecting them on schedule the day after tomorrow!"

For the rest of that day and the next Lambert worked feverishly to completely enclose the house with palm bark except for door and window openings. The news soon spread to every home on the lake that the white man's wife and baby were coming soon.

Lambert watched across the silver and gold sunlight on the lake that happy afternoon as a moving speck in the sky grew larger and homed in on the lake. Splashing onto the water, the plane taxied up and docked in front of the new house as wide-eyed Indians ran up to join the excitement.

The Ticunas quickly thronged around Doris, almost as delighted as Lambert to see her and the little blond Betsy. A few of them dared to reach out and touch Doris's arm and hair as if they expected her to feel different from them. She responded with smiles and a few Ticuna syllables, indicating her happiness at arriving. She had to hold tight to Betsy to keep her little "muneca"—golden-haired doll —from being swept out of her arms. Welcome home!

Early Bible translation. (Don Hesse)

Chapter Five **PIONEERING**

Doris looked up at the leaf-roofed, bark-walled house on stilts and suddenly became aware that there were no doors or shutters. Inside there were no screens or ceiling or walls. Their future ceiling, a large piece of cheesecloth, draped to serve as a mosquito netting against the myriad insects as well as other nightly visitors such as rats and vampire bats. There was no furniture yet—only a floor to hold their air mattresses for sleeping. Almost like Jungle Camp! Doris was glad she had been there first.

July 29, 1953, was a new beginning for Lambert and Doris Anderson. Together they watched the JAARS plane take off and tried to imagine what it would be like to stay in the jungle six months, far from any white civilization. They knew a quick adaptation to Ticuna culture would smooth the way.

The daily radio communications with Yarinacocha were a boon. A Wisconsin friend, Clyde Spaulding, had provided the equipment, and it served faithfully except for a brief spell when an antenna relay failed. Lambert fixed it the next day with wood, nails, and strips from a tin can, and radio contact was restored.

A door of split palm strips was made and hung about a week after Doris' arrival. Narrow wooden slats were nailed across the window openings to give a semblance of enclosure. Bark walls kept out most intruders from the nearby jungle, but not the neighbor's cat, a frequent visitor. Tiny ants were a problem around the dining table, but a moat of tuna-fish cans under the legs of the table turned them away.

The bed and benches were built from axe-hewn boards obtained from the Indians. Some shelves and a table were made from used packing crate lumber, and chairs were later brought from Yarinacocha. One of the packing boxes made by Lambert's father served as a sturdy desk for translation study. The other boxes with attached hinges became kitchen cupboards. A large Indian hammock hung from the rafters in a corner of the living room. The rustic dwelling was taking on a touch of luxury!

The "visitor's bench" seldom lacked occupants. It almost appeared that visiting children had been sent to keep a continual watch on the white man's family. They loved to leaf through old magazines—backwards and forwards and often upside down. Appreciative "Ducaxes" (look at this) with out-thrust lower lips signaled new opportunities for word pickups to Doris. Sometimes the children watched silently from the bench, their eyes wide with wonderment and curiosity, followed by staccato inquiries.

It was not unusual for the onlookers to fall asleep on their favorite bench. Rather than send them home to a raucous drinking party, Doris often covered them with a blanket for the night. Morning revealed the blanket folded neatly and the children slipped away before the Andersons were up.

The arrival of "army ants" was another story. They came in the night, awakening the Andersons with their rustling advance in the kitchen. The floor was a black moving mass as the ants proceeded toward the bedroom. Lambert sprayed the legs of their big bed while Doris brought Betsy from her crib to their ant-free island and they waited out the twenty-minute invasion until the army passed through the house and continued in the direction of Pablo's house—who with neither bed nor bug spray might soon be climbing his guayava tree.

Doris and Lambert counted an average of four drunken parties on the lake each week. Empty rum bottles and machetes became vicious weapons for friends-turned-enemies after a few drinks of mind-crazing liquor. Pacifying the wild-eyed brawlers was not only difficult but sometimes impossible.

"Please come, Mr. White Man; my father hit my mother with his fist and now my mother's chasing him around the house with a machete!" was one plea.

"Mrs. White Lady, do you have some sugar to make my brother vomit?" asked an anxious boy. "He took barbasco poison because they're all drunk and my mother told him he was a no-good!"

"Look, Lambert," called Doris another time. "Here come two policemen and the Indians are chasing them. The Ticunas are dead drunk and it looks like they're trying to take away the officers' guns!"

As the outnumbered police took refuge on the porch of the Andersons' house, Lambert and Doris stood on each side of the stairs and shoved off Indian pursuers as they tried to come up the steps. Indian women, more sober than their husbands, tried to pull their men back, reminding them that their punishment awaited them in the district jail. At last the women's pleading prevailed and the angry mob began to disperse. The policemen, grateful to the Andersons, were able to return to Caballococha with no further trouble.

Lambert found that subsistence in the jungle can become a full-time job, and he needed to finish the house and simple pieces of furniture. But he remembered Uncle Cam's advice: "Try to get in at least one hour of language work every day. No matter how much you have to do on the house, don't let a day go by without working on the language."

Language work, indeed, was the reason they were there. Every syllable of learning was vitally important—and sometimes difficult, "How do you say, 'yes,' Miguel?" Lambert asked. "Ngü," he said. (Ü is pronounced somewhat like 'oo' of book.)

"I mean, 'okay,' " Lambert persisted.

"Ngü," he repeated.

Thinking the answer simply meant, "What did you say?" Lambert tried "How do you say, 'It is affirmative'?"

And Miguel repeated "Ngü" emphatically. "That is what we say in our language." The grunting sound was the Ticuna word for "Yes."

Words and phrases heard frequently were written on flashcards for quick checking. And they were needed! One day Pablo came over for a visit and Lambert confidently greeted him and invited him to be seated. Pablo responded, "Yes, I'm leaving right now." He shooked Lambert's hand and walked out the door. Lambert seized his flash cards and discovered that instead of saying "Sit down" he had used the similar term for "Are you going now?"

The Andersons tried to make language-learning enjoyable as well as systematic. When the Indians laughed at their absurd mistakes, the chagrined missionaries probed for the humor and joined in the laughter. Sometimes when the joviality turned to mockery, the newcomers retaliated by serving up a phonetic teaser like "railroad." Since the Ticunas have no words beginning with "r" and no "l's" in their language, and every word ends in a vowel, the Ticuna version came out something like "waywo"—a big laugh from the original.

Doris found a welcome break from language study each day by creative planning in the kitchen. The Indians' daily diet of bananas, yucca, and fish was monotonous to the new residents of the jungle, and until the boat came from Yarinacocha they had only a bit of salt, sugar, oil, and oatmeal to supplement the native diet. After three weeks the boat still failed to appear; then six weeks passed and Betsy's milk supply was nearly exhausted.

The baby had gone from powdered to evaporated to condensed milk, and eight different kinds were used in three weeks as anything available was bought in Caballococha. One day in September they got down to the last two cans.

"We must get some milk for the baby," Doris reminded

Lambert as he turned on the radio for their morning call to Yarinacocha.

"A plane is traveling north today to supply translators in the Iquitos area," advised the base operator. "Call back at 5:30 if you need a flight."

Iquitos was two hundred miles away, but milk was imperative. At 5:30 Lambert radioed the pilot in Iquitos for an emergency flight. At that moment a knock sounded on the door and an Indian entered with a message. It was a note from Carlos Saenz, a merchant in Caballococha, notifying them that their food shipment had arrived.

"Just a minute," Lambert checked the pilot. "We've just received word our shipment is in Caballococha. There's no need to come now—praise the Lord!" God's timing accounted for baby milk as well as radio generators.

Doris was flustered by the sudden wealth in food cans and packages, but her pleasant predicament dissolved in the discovery that the drums containing food had evidently toppled into the water somewhere on their journey and the boxes of jello and pudding were soaked while bags of flour resembled concrete blocks. With determination and a hammer she found the flour could be broken into chunks and rubbed through a sifter for baking purposes. Fresh bread and fruit pies became their family treat.

As the season changed, the Andersons discovered new foods in Indian homes. There were many varieties of bananas, including the plantain which was called the "bread of Loreto," the state in which Cushillococha is located. Yucca was fried, baked, and boiled, and a toasted form called "farina" could be stored for long periods.

Watermelons grew on the Amazon beaches during the low water season, and many fruits thrived including a kind of grape growing on trees. A large papaya weighed thirteen pounds and a magnificent pineapple fifteen. Most of the fruits and vegetables were sterilized with soap and water; the easiest way to clean pineapple was to flame it over the two-burner kerosene stove.

One day the Andersons heard a wild party at the next

house a hundred yards away. Soon running footsteps and a loud voice announced a visitor outside. "That white man pays us badly. I work hard and he pays me a poor price," complained the wavering voice.

It was Alfonso, the man who had sold Lambert two warped, poorly hewn boards for the house. Doris urged Lambert to keep out of sight to avoid antagonizing the drunk assailant, and she watched Alfonso stumble back and forth across the yard, gesturing toward the house and ranting against the white man. Then he let out a shriek and turned back to his party. Would he get others and return? Something quieted him down, however, and nothing more was heard for several hours.

Then another Indian knocked on the door and Doris looked out cautiously. It was a Ticuna whose hands had been snapped off by an alligator he mistook for log when he was returning home from a drinking party. He swung his stubbed arms aimlessly as he came through the door and advised in slurred tones: "Don't be afraid. I haven't come to kill you; just want to teach you my language." Whereupon he started saying words and asked Doris to repeat them. She was a very cooperative student that session, and apparently pleased her mentor.

On Christmas afternoon the Anderson yard was festive with laughter of Ticuna children playing drop-the-handkerchief. A Christmas tree made from branches of a lemon tree was gaily decorated with paper ornaments and pictures cut from old cards. Refreshments were cold lemonade and popcorn—a tasty innovation for the Ticuna children. Adults had been invited too, but they preferred a drunken double-header at two homes hosting the entire village. As Doris and Lambert listened to the carousing, they yearned for the day when the Ticunas' would celebrate the coming of God's Son to earth with the gift of lasting joy.

As Lambert worked day by day with a language helper, Doris wrote down household terms she obtained from Pablo's daughter Chuira and added them to their fund of knowledge.

"Lambert, I'm getting more and more words that are identical pairs," Doris observed from time to time. "Although Chuira insists they're different, I can't hear any difference between them. The words seem to have exactly the same vowels and consonants." Then one day she came to his desk and remarked, "You know, I'm afraid we have a tone language here!"

Lambert put down his pen and turned toward her. "No, Doris, you must be mistaken. They've told us it's very unlikely that there are any tone languages in Peru. Maybe it's just a problem of accent. Try checking it out for stress. This just *can't* be a tone language!"

The January days grew longer and longer, and the end of their six month's stint neared. More than change from their jungle surroundings, the Andersons needed linguistic advice at the base. A Ticuna Indian and his wife would accompany them to continue language study.

On February 11 the JAARS Norseman dipped over the lake and landed to take the Andersons back to Yarinacocha. Their departure was sad and happy—and recognized as a brief trip away from "home." Winging into the linguists' base of twenty homes at Yarinacocha was a thrilling experience. At last they could talk English again with everyone in sight! Little Betsy cried when the whiteskinned strangers reached for her; she already missed her dark-skinned friends.

A few days after arrival the Andersons were able to consult with veteran linguist Don Stark, who had helped translate the New Testament into Mixteco, a complicated tone language of Mexico. He listened to some of the contrasting word pairs pronounced by Amanico, the Ticuna informant, and mused, "There does seem to be tonal differences here. It's very possible that you do have significant meaningful tone in the language."

Lambert hated to admit it, but this giant obstacle looked like the kind of progress he had to face with the Ticunas.

Spraying rubber trees. The Ticunas, who traditionally have worked wild rubber trees, now have one of the few rubber plantations in the area. (Lambert Anderson)

Chapter Six **DETOURS**

Amanico's outgoing personality enhanced his value as a language helper at Yarinacocha—when he was sober. Often Lambert would work at his desk for hours before Amanico appeared with an apology and explanation: a bad headache had required his hammock for extra rest. A little investigation traced the incapacity to a drinking fiesta the night before in a nearby village. If Satan had fashioned a special snare for the Ticunas, it was intoxicating drink. The problems and needs of the spiritually bereft tribe stirred the Yarinacocha Christians to concerted prayer for Cushillococha.

One morning Amanico's wife came running excitedly to the Anderson's house: "Mr. White Man, they've taken my husband. He doesn't have a paper."

Amanico had been picked up by the local authorities because he didn't have a draft registration card required by law. Consequently he was liable for military service.

Lambert and fellow worker Bob Wacker drove their Jeep through rutted trails to Pucallpa and found the proper official. They explained the situation earnestly: Amanico was a key man needed for language work, and he didn't have a draft card because his father had never obtained the required birth certificate for him. The official asked several questions, then to Lambert's relief agreed to sign a release.

Setbacks and breakthroughs, delays and discoveries— the days passed swiftly and the Andersons found themselves restless to return to Cushillococha. On schedule, they arrived in August and felt that they were coming home.

There had been no way to lock up their house—they had simply piled their belongings in a back corner and invited Alejandro, a young Ticuna, to live there with his family and care for things. It had been a pointed display of confidence since the Indian could have easily taken everything and skipped across the border.

Any misgivings were quelled as Alejandro stood smiling to welcome them home. Undisturbed cobwebs covered their possessions—the Indian family hadn't even touched the half empty box of cereal Doris had said they could eat. Alejandro assured them with pride that everything was just as he had received it.

"It's great to be back among the people again," Lambert radioed. He sensed a mutual love and trust growing between his family and the short, wiry Indians with their high cheek bones, straight black hair, and sharpened front teeth.

Betsy was like a ray of sunshine in the village. She responded with obvious delight as the Indian children showered her with attention. Ticunas, young and old, were frequent visitors to the Andersons' home.

On a Monday afternoon drums began a staccato beat, and Amanico invited Lambert to his niece's "coming out party," her initiation into womanhood. Through the night and following day, the incessant drumbeat heralded the festivities.

On Tuesday about midnight, a glistening full moon illuminated the scene as Indians gathered close to watch the star of the drama escorted from a makeshift enclosure behind the communal house. She was painted black from head to foot and wore a swatch of red cloth around her hips. A profuse array of bird bills, beetle wings, monkey teeth, and snail shells hung around her neck. On her head was a spectacular bark-cloth crown bedecked with red and blue parrot feathers interspersed with tufts of white down.

Ten or twelve women and girls joined arms on either side of her and rows of women stepped behind as they all began a marching dance around the inside, then the outside, of the pavilion-like structure.

Through the night the dignified procession continued—four steps forward, two steps back, four steps forward, two steps back—all in rhythm to the driving beat of the drums and the clatter of nutshells on a rattle stick thumped on the ground.

Shortly after daybreak several women screamed and bolted toward the girl. In the melee the girl was surrounded and pulled away from the building. "The demons—they've come to attack her," shrieked the women.

Fifteen or twenty bark-cloth-clad creatures burst out of a nearby thicket, brandishing long spears and brightly decorated bark-cloth shields. Their faces were covered with hooded masks made of carved balsa wood, their ugly features accentuated by red and black dyes and glittering insets of metal. After repeated mock attempts to capture the girl they suddenly whirled and fled in seeming defeat.

Early Wednesday morning the drums and dancing stopped. The girl was then seated on a bark-cloth mat, the first time she had been allowed to sit down since midnight, and given a cup of rum to drink. Six women seated themselves around her. As her uncle supported her exhausted body, the women began to pluck out her hair—several strands at a time, with a quick snap close to the scalp.

As the aggravating pain became more painful, the girl made attempts to escape. This signaled a need for more rum-sedation to be poured into her. Eventually another uncle was called to help hold the bleeding, moaning girl, and after an hour all her hair had been pulled out. Now she was eligible for marriage.

Tribal ceremonies enabled the Andersons to deepen friendships with the Ticunas as well as to expand their knowledge of the language. In the midst of the community activities and inevitable distractions, Lambert and Doris pursued their main task.

Part of their strategy was to memorize twenty new words

or useful expressions each day, in addition to reviewing previously studied terms. "Each flash card," thought Doris, "is a link in the chain that will some day give us fluency in the Ticuna language."

In July an emergency loomed. Doris was threatened by a miscarriage, and needed special care in Yarinacocha. The larger Catalina, a gift to the Institute in Peru from the government of Mexico, would come to take Doris for medical help. As it was now low-water season on the lake, the deepest area had to be marked off with white flags for the Catalina to land safely.

On board with the pilot were Uncle Cam and Elaine, solicitous and encouraging in this anxious time. That afternoon Lambert saw Uncle Cam in the yard talking to Pablo. The literature crusader was showing the Indians words in a small primer and saying in Spanish: "Some day, Pablo, you're going to be able to read in your own language." Pablo nodded noncommittally, and Lambert wondered how far away this impossible seeming goal was.

The next day they carried Doris on a stretcher to a large canoe and then paddled to the Catalina anchored in the middle of the lake. While she received careful attention in Yarinacocha, Lambert would be aided temporarily by another linguist, Bob Wacker. Language study continued, but it was a daily testing time for Lambert to be separated from his ill wife.

In early October Lambert was informed Doris must go to Lima for more expert medical help, and he should accompany her. Regretfully closing his notebooks, Lambert was soon on a plane to Yarinacocha.

Two days later Lambert and Doris were winging toward Lima, but medical science was not to have the final word in this case. That night the Anderson's first son, Keith, was born two months prematurely and he lived only a few hours.

The parents could not help but wonder why this life had been given and then taken so quickly, but as Lambert sought solace in God's Word he came to Psalm 18:30—"As for God, his way is perfect"—and his heart was satisfied with the answer. The next day, while visiting Doris in the hospital, she told him the Lord had given her a strengthening verse—"As for God, his way is perfect," and the grieving parents were thrilled to learn how God had spoken to each with the same voice.

At a simple funeral attended by a few close friends, Lambert stood with bowed head as an Indian Christian of the Piro tribe prayed at the grave, "Lord, give them another son. No—two more sons!" It was a prayer God would honor.

The Institute was in need of a buyer in Lima to purchase and ship supplies to the jungle base, and Lambert and Doris needed more practice in Spanish, the national language of Peru, so the Andersons received this temporary assignment while Doris convalesced.

The new post had its trials also. "Is Senor Azula there?" inquired Lambert on a business call before identifying himself—by name, that is. A secretary's twitter was followed by a giggled announcement to a companion: "It's the man from the Instituto Linguistico."

A traumatic moment came one day when Colonel Carlos Moya, chief of staff of the Air Force, called for a certain clarification. As Jerry Elder, Lima coordinator, was out of the Institute office, Lambert was the only man available with the answer. But that telephone seemed charged with 2,000 volts of electricity as far as Lambert was concerned, and a secretary coaxed for a full minute before convincing him to pick it up. Fortunately, Colonel Moya was a very understanding man and later became a close friend.

Gradually Spanish became more and more familiar, and by the end of a seven-month stint in Lima, Lambert and Doris were both conversing comfortably with Peruvian friends.

Leonardo reading to his daughters Viri and Quelina. (Leo Lance)

Chapter Seven BREAKTHROUGH

To the Ticunas, the Andersons had been away a long time. What had happened? Were they ever coming back?

Indeed—the delay was also in God's timetable. In April of 1955 Lambert, Doris, and Betsy returned home to a rousing welcome. Eager hands struggled with heavy cases of food as the plane was unloaded, and the Ticunas' recurring question: "How long can you stay?" was answered again and again: "A long time!"

Lilia, a friendly, intelligent teen-ager, became Doris' helper. Her mother's house at the far end of the lake was one of the neatest homes in the village. Lilia assisted with household chores—washing, cleaning, and cooking—but her main task was to care for Betsy, by now an active toddler.

One morning Lilia took Betsy with her in a canoe on the nearby stream to wash clothes. Betsy amused herself in one end of the canoe, splashing in the water and imitating Lilia by soaping and scrubbing her doll. In the midst of her washing, Lilia casually looked up and saw a mass of blond hair floating away on the surface of the water.

Panic-stricken, she realized that Betsy was drowning. Plunging into the water, Lilia grabbed Betsy's hair and pulled the gasping child out. Betsy's wailing mourned the loss of her vanished doll as well as announcing her fright.

Lilia was still trembling when she reached the house with Betsy in her arms. Quaveringly she recounted the incident and cried: "What if I hadn't looked up just then?" Shaken by this brush with tragedy Lilia vowed, "never again to take 'Bechi' near the water!"

The Ticuna girl was a constant supply of new language material, and she was especially helpful with pitch. Determining whether this really was a tonal language was becoming a primary objective for Doris. What were the clues they could follow to unravel the intricate patterns of varying tones?

"Listen to this, Lam," Doris said one day. "You say *oxta* with a low tone on the second syllable and it means 'lisa fish'; you say the same word with a high tone on that syllable and it means 'brain.' Also, here's the word, *chanaxü*—'I put it'; and *chanaxü*—'I make it.' It appears that by changing the pitch on the last vowel, one can determine whether it means 'I put it' or 'I make it.' I'm finding dozens of these minimal pairs now. The only way I can explain them all is that we must have a tonal language."

As they continued to work over new materials they found more and more words that were identical except for differences in vowel pitch. It was a shock they were reluctantly getting accustomed to.

With her musical background, Doris found that the easiest way to indicate the pitches on words was by using the letter names such as C-D-E. Wouldn't it be fun to try playing Ticuna on the accordion? One day she said to a group of visitors: "Listen to this and tell me what it says." She played on the accordion E-E-E-D-A-G-D-E-D-D-E-C. They looked puzzled until she said, "Wūxi ya yatü yea coyaxü nadau" (a man saw an alligator over there). Then she repeated it on the accordion and their eyes grew big with astonishment and they broke into unconstrained laughter. "Yes, that's just the way we say it," they agreed.

Another teen-ager was to help the Andersons significantly. She visited the missionaries with her cousin Dochia to swim off the raft in their port. Dochia's name was easy to pronounce, but the second girl's name was so difficult that Doris nicknamed her "Pretty Girl," and she was one of the prettiest Indian girls they had seen.

Early one morning word arrived that Pretty Girl had been badly beaten. In a furious outburst of anger her father had mercilessly slapped her with the broad side of a machete. She was badly bruised and her hands had several deep cuts. A deep gash in her side and hip were already infected when her mother arrived at the Anderson's house to ask for medicine.

The incident was reported to government authorities, and when they could not find the father to take him to jail they insisted that Pretty Girl and her mother go with them. As the group passed the Andersons' home the mother pled for help from the missionaries. "How can we go with them when we don't understand what they're saying to us, and we don't know how to tell them anything?"

After a brief consultation with Lambert, Doris suggested the authorities leave the girl in her care. She could stay on their closed-in front porch. To the mother's great relief, the policemen gave their consent.

In a few days Pretty Girl was able to walk with little pain and seemed to want to help Doris in some way to show her appreciation. What would she be like as a language helper? To Doris' delight, Pretty Girl spoke with unusual clarity, emphasizing the tones so that they could be heard easily. And on request she would either speak a word at normal speed or drag it out slowly, enabling Doris to hear the pitches like a musical phrase. "Thank you, Lord, for sending us Pretty Girl," Doris rejoiced.

Both Lambert and Doris realized they were making definite progress in the language analysis. Several weeks later the evidence seemed to be conclusive as Doris and Pretty Girl had been working and reworking lists of words with contrasting pitches. "Lam, on the basis of these lists of words, I'm convinced that we have *five* tones in Ticuna."

Lambert was stunned. That was a staggering possibility. Could they confirm it to the linguistic experts? Were they finally on the right track—?

"Dr. Pike is to visit here this fall," announced the

Yarinacocha radio operator one morning. "We're setting up a workshop for all those who are interested."

"Great!" Lambert replied, "we'll start lining up the materials."

With repeated checking, long sheets of linguistic data were fairly well organized by the time a JAARS plane came to take the Andersons, Lilia, and Pretty Girl to the base for the workshop with Dr. Kenneth Pike, the Wycliffe consultant-professor from the University of Michigan.

On his first afternoon at Yarinacocha, Dr. Pike listened to Pretty Girl's clear pronunciation of the contrasting pitches in the lists of words Doris had prepared. All the linguists at the base were present to hear Dr. Pike analyze and determine the significant sounds in the language—especially listening for tone.

Going up and down the columns of Ticuna words and phrases he carefully made comparisons. After listening to the material for about an hour, he concluded, "I postulate that you have a language here with at least four significant levels of pitch, and perhaps five!"

After a number of sessions with the Andersons and the Ticuna informants, Dr. Pike concluded that Ticuna has five significant levels in the tonal structure, plus four glides from one tone to another!

"Apply arithmetic to this situation," Lambert elaborated, "and we have here a theoretical possibility of fifty-four vowels! This is by the fact that the six vowels in the language are multiplied by nine possibilities of tone. Plus that, many of the vowels can be nasalized or laryngelized, and sometimes both!"

It was staggering—particularly after accepting the early theory that there were no tonal languages in Peru! But the Andersons knew God had made both the Ticunas' tongue and the missionaries' brain—for clear communication between them.

Some of the early Ticuna deacons: Pachi, Jose, Chico, Carlos, Cuere, Alberto, Leonardo, Liborio, and Agustin. (Lambert Anderson)

Chapter Eight **BROTHERS!**

"The Piro Indians are praying for the Ticunas," translator Esther Matteson informed Lambert one day. She reported that Antlers, the Piro leader who had prayed for the Andersons at the graveside in Lima a year earlier, was now praying for the entire Ticuna tribe.

"Lord, turn them around; show them the right trail. Help them to trust in you!" was the nature of Antlers's confident request. With such simple, humble faith, Antlers and the Andersons seemed assured a definite answer. Lambert and Doris began to anticipate the Ticunas' response to God's truth in oral form. Until now they had been engrossed in language analysis as the presentation of a detailed write-up on basic sounds and the grammar systems of Ticuna was required before translation work could begin.

Cushillococha village was astir in May of 1956 with the news that a "God's Word-teller" from the White Man's land had just arrived. Pastor J. B. Windle of the Oconto church of Lambert's boyhood had come to visit for a few days.

Betsy was excited about showing "Uncle Jack" around the village and introducing him to her friends. His open friendliness inspired instant trust. Surely his words would be true.

It was a time of refreshing for Lambert and Doris as they caught up on news from the United States. And a time of enlightenment as Pastor Jack discovered the jungle.

One evening as they talked over a cup of coffee, the visitor's eyes widened as a three-inch cockroach climbed over the edge of the table and advanced fearlessly. Striving for casualness, Jack took the saucer from under his cup and turned it upside down over the cockroach. But his astonishment could not be hidden when the saucer started to "walk" off the table on the roach's back!

Pastor Windle and the Andersons prayed often for God's leading in the meetings they planned for the coming week. When the appointed evening came, short logs were brought in and topped with planks for their guests in the Anderson's living room and front porch. "You preach and I'll interpret," Lambert said.

Adults and youngsters climbed the steps on the Andersons' house and found places on the benches, soon filling them. Others had to sit on the floor. Kerosene lamps cast shadows on their curious faces as they sat quietly waiting for words about God.

As Pastor Windle spoke a sentence, Lambert translated it into Ticuna as best he could. Doris followed with simple flannelboard depictions emphasizing the central points of Pastor Windle's sermon. The get-togethers continued each evening through the week.

In his last meeting, Pastor Windle reviewed the Bible's basic message—God loves man, man has rebelled against God, Christ died for man's sinful rebellion so man can be forgiven and have eternal life. He closed with clear words about the meaning of Christ's cross. Then Doris illustrated the crucifixion story, prepared with the help of Pretty Girl. The Indians were deeply impressed with the flannelgraph figures, especially the largest one of Christ on the cross —the price God paid for man's salvation. Would anyone in the audience understand the message and receive Christ?

In the hush of late evening three Ticunas lingered after everyone else had gone: Jose, outspoken leader in the village; his wife Wae; and Lilia. "We want to receive the gift of God," they stated simply. And the three of them knelt with the three white men and prayed, acknowledging their sins and asking Christ for forgiveness and new life.

Through words and pictures, the first Ticunas had heard

God speak and become spiritual brothers and sisters in God's eternal family.

Pastor Windle's advice to the Andersons as he left was: "Do something special for the children—start a Sunday school and have some clubs for the young people. The adults will come later."

Accordingly Doris and Lambert set up Sunday school on their front porch, teaching Bible stories which Lilia helped to translate—The Lost Sheep, the Prodigal Son, the Good Samaritan. . . .

Sunday school began with fifteen or twenty, but increased to fifty and sixty before long. By opening the front door wide, the porch and front room could be used as one big enclosure for both Sunday school and Sunday evening meetings.

In addition to translating simple Bible stories for Sunday school, Doris and Lilia worked together on choruses. Doris remembered helping Bob Longacre write down Trique songs, but composing new melodies or altering known ones to conform to the tones of Ticuna words without distorting their meaning was a new test.

"Jesus Loves Me," "Into My Heart," and "In My Father's House" were completed. The music was necessarily different—and for the most part was barely recognizable to Spanish or English singers. For example:

Si - lent night, ho - ly night.

Na-mex-ē-chi ga chü-tex-ü̈ rü na-chi-pe-tü ga chü-tax-ü.

The only other Ticuna songs known were the chants of the teen-age girls' coming-out parties, or dirges at funerals.

Remembering the rest of Pastor Windle's advice, Lambert and Doris started a "club" for older children. New songs and stories on Christian growth accompanied "fun times" of games and handcraft projects. One by one, young people trusted in Christ, and by the end of the year almost twenty had believed—most of them the first Christians in their families.

"We're doing fairly well at carrying on a conversation with the Ticunas, and we can buy and sell in the language," the Andersons noted gratefully—"so why don't we try some simple Scripture translation?"

There was one problem—Amancio had gone back to the river to work in his garden, and other language helpers didn't seem to have the ability the Andersons needed.

"Why don't you try working with the new Ticuna that's come from across the Colombian border to marry Maricuta?" Doris suggested one day. "They call him Pachi, and they say he's gone to Spanish school for several years. Maybe with a little help he could learn to write his own language."

A few days later Lambert reported, "This Pachi is unbelievable!"

Lambert had asked him to write down the Ticuna equivalent of "I weave it"—*chanamu*. "Now write 'I spear it,'" Lambert directed. Again he wrote *chanamu*. "And now write, 'I send it.'" Once again Pachi wrote *chanamu*. "But you've written the same word three times," protested Lambert. "Are they all the same?"

"Oh, no sir," Pachi replied quickly. "Those words are all different, but in our language you don't write the difference—you can only *hear* the difference when you speak it."

Lambert then explained the way pitched levels could be indicated by writing numbers above each vowel. The highest pitch was written with a number "1" and they went down to the lowest written with number "5."

Lilia came to work early one morning and since the door

was not open at Andersons' house she continued down the trail to visit Pretty Girl and her husband. The missionaries heard her screaming unintelligibly as she came running back. Her words tumbled out in wild confusion and Doris had to shake her to calm her down enough to find out what had happened. Pretty Girl had eaten barbasco poison in a fit of anger.

"She was jerking up the roots by the handful and chewing them when I got there," Lilia sobbed.

As Lambert and Doris started down the trail, they met her husband coming toward them carrying Pretty Girl over his shoulder. She was already delirious and all efforts to save her were futile. Within twenty minutes she was dead. "God, where is our Pretty Girl now?" agonized the Andersons. Had she understood the crucifixion and resurrection stories of Jesus she had helped to translate and inwardly trusted in Jesus?

Evidently the husband wanted to go to a fiesta on the Amazon River and Pretty Girl told him she didn't want to go. He told her to get his white pants ready and he would go himself, and she refused, saying that the last time he had been flirting with another girl. He shoved her and she tripped and fell down. Infuriated, she got up screaming threats to take poison. He didn't believe her, so had not followed her into the woods where Lilia found her. Uncontrolled anger had victimized another Ticuna, and a precious one.

As Lambert worked with Pachi, he realized more and more his helper's exceptional abilities. Pachi soon learned to write the pitch levels on the syllables using the numbers.

Most new words had to be compared with known ones in order to establish whether the pitches were higher, lower, or the same. This was done by comparing a substitution list such as: "one dog"; "one cat"; "one man"; etc. Since pitch of "one" was already known, the tone levels of the new words could be readily determined.

Pachi became so adept at writing the tones that Lambert

could give him whole pages of text to mark. One day he proved his acuteness when Lambert called to Doris, "What are the tones on this new work?" and Pachi spoke up before she could answer: "1-5" in English!

"Who's going to be the best translator," Lambert thought, "myself or this sharp Ticuna?" It was exciting to select New Testament verses and narratives and translate them into Ticuna.

But it wasn't long before they encountered some formidable hurdles rising from the terms in a foreign culture. "How can we say, 'cornerstone,' Doris? The only stones these people know of are brought from hundreds of miles away by boat, sold by weight, and only used for sharpening machetes." After thinking it over a bit, they decided on the words for "main supporting post."

"How would you say 'fathers,' meaning 'ancestors'?" Lambert asked Pachi.

"The Ticuna word oxi means 'grandfather,' and we use that same word for 'great-grandfather' or 'great-great-grandfather.' We don't have a word for 'ancestors'," he answered.

"Could you say 'our long-ago grandfather'?" Lambert suggested.

"Perfect."

Betsy was speaking fluently in Ticuna at three years of age. It was her first language, spoken when playing alone with her dolls. About three o'clock one afternoon Lilia burst into the translators' room and called, "Bechi's gone; I can't find her."

Language work came to a sudden halt.

"Where was she last, Lilia?" Doris asked.

"Right out in the yard."

"Who was she with?"

"She was just playing by herself."

"Xaxya, has Bechi been here?"

"No, I haven't seen her."

"Pablo, have you seen Bechi?"

"No, I just came in from fishing."

Lambert and Doris walked the trail from one end to the other—both upstream and downstream, anxiously asking everyone they met.

"Lambert, it's going to be dark before long. What can we do if she's still not here?"

"I don't know, unless we get some of the men together and take lanterns out on the trails into the jungle. She can't have gone very far. Didn't you say you saw her about an hour and a half ago?"

"Yes, but she could be a long way off in that time."

"Chuira, did Bechi go by here?"

"I don't know, I just came up from cleaning fish in the port."

"Lord, you see our little girl. Please take care of her," Lambert prayed.

A full two hours passed and Lambert and Doris were feeling desperate about their lost daughter. Where else could they look? Who could they ask? As they tried to decide what to do next, Lilia came running up to them. "They've found her! Eca found her in the garden out in the jungle. Teadura took her along to eat sugar cane."

The Andersons rushed over in time to see a small procession coming down the trail from the jungle, the Indian children carrying bananas on their heads and stalks of sugar cane over their shoulders. And a blond Indian, Betsy, tagging along at the end with a length of sugar cane over her shoulder. Bechi spoke Ticuna too well!

As the translators worked together, the subject of superstition and the local witchdoctor came up from time to time. Lambert suggested that the medicine man's power was more imagined than real.

Pachi's vehement rejounder startled Lambert. "Don't think that way! I know. That man has power you don't dream of. He has his own armies, airplanes, speed boats, and can send darts of chonta palm wood hundreds of miles to cause sickness to the person he wants to harm."

Questioned further, Pachi related his own experience. "The witchdoctor told me to stay here and not go back to

Colombia. I didn't listen to him and we moved back to where I lived before. Two weeks later my only son suddenly became sick and died. It was the punishment of the witchdoctor because I didn't obey him."

The power was very real as far as Pachi was concerned, and his opinion was shared by all the village. Divina, one of Taybücü's three wives, told in great detail of a relative who had become very sick as the result of a hex by a witchdoctor.

It seemed that all adversity was blamed on curses by witchdoctors—people got sick, accidents occurred, death struck. To get well from an illness, the only way was said to be the help of another witchdoctor who would tell you for a fee who was the cause of the affliction. For an additional fee he would smoke his ceremonial pipe and with great ritual draw out the chonta palm darts that supposedly were causing the pain.

One night shortly after darkness had fallen a man arrived with the news: "Deu has speared himself."

The teen-ager had gone fishing with his assortment of spears—the light, metal-tipped cane lances for small fish and the heavy harpoon with a long cord attached for spearing twenty-pound gamitanas. Ordinarily the lances are stabbed into the side of the canoe as a safeguard, but this time Deu had left one lying beside him as he paddled along. Seeing a big fish jump, he quickly stood up and hurled the heavy harpoon and as the cord sizzled out it snagged in the lance and drove it into Deu's wrist.

The Indians had gathered around in the yard by the light of a small kerosene flame when Lambert arrived. The only solution was to tear the spear out, they said.

Realizing that the metal barbs were caught behind the tendons and that Deu's hand could be crippled for life if they were torn, Lambert administered several shots of novocaine and urged: "We'll have to take him to the doctor in Caballococha. It's the only way we'll save his hand. Get your lantern ready and I'll go with you."

Three hours over logs, under low branches, through swampy areas, and across log bridges were rewarded by the glimpse of a small light burning in the hospital. Dr. Moura was still up writing letters.

After a quick examination he administered more shots of anesthetic and then unwrapped his sterilized surgical instruments. With a deft scalpel he was able to work through to the barbs of the metal tip, then as he pushed the tendons out of the way, Lambert pulled and worked the tip loose. Several sutures later the incision was closed, and Deu was assured use of his hand again.

The following afternoon at the translation table the subject was discussed by Pachi.

"You think that just happened to Deu, don't you? That wasn't an accident. What really took place is that a witch-doctor from the Cocama tribe wanted to spend the night at Deu's home. His father wouldn't let him stay there, and this was the witchdoctor's retaliation!"

That topic remained unsettled, but the language work continued. Scriptures and Christian messages were translated and rechecked for presentation on Sunday nights. During the following months eight more Ticuna men came forward to surrender their hearts to the Lord. Among them were Pablo and Pretty Girl's father. This was a year of bountiful first fruits—God was speaking Ticuna in clear tones.

By December the Andersons were back in Yarinacocha accompanied by Pachi and his wife for further translation work.

On December 20, 1956, Lambert Lyle Anderson II was born. Before long Betsy had little "Bert" in her doll buggy, and she offered to let him keep "Nancy Baby," her favorite doll.

It was also in December that Pachi opened his heart to Jesus while listening to Lambert explain the Christmas story! What a glorious year!

Entering 1957 a dominant goal was the translation of

selected verses about the life of Christ. Pachi and Lambert translated them as accurately as they could and then began memorizing them one by one as part of their moments of meditation prior to starting the work of the day.

Now that Pachi loved the Lord, he was eager to serve him—not just the Andersons. And serving God set his whole life on course, moving forward to the purpose of the Eternal One.

Filed teeth have long been a distinguishing mark of the Ticunas. The teeth are actually chipped with a knife, rather than filed. (Don Hesse)

Chapter Nine **FREEDOM**

Santa Rita is a small town one hundred and fifty miles downstream from Cushillococha on the north bank of the Amazon River in Brazil. Missionaries of the Association of Baptists for World Evangelism started church services there for the Portuguese-speaking Brazilians, but little by little Ticuna Indians began attending the church. After a while Miguel, an Indian leader, was asked to interpret the sermon in Ticuna so the monolingual women and children could also understand the message.

In 1957 the missionaries planned a series of meetings in the Ticuna language and invited the Andersons and Pachi to participate. Government documents were secured for the border crossing and plans were laid to make the trip in June.

The Ticunas anticipated the arrival of the blond North American who had been studying their language, but it was Pachi who galvanized their attention. Using the newly translated Scripture portions, Pachi introduced Christ as a personal friend that he himself had come to know and love.

Many Brazilian Ticunas were ready to make personal decisions, and they followed Pachi's example that week. The language helper had become God's evangelist!

On their way home from Santa Rita, the Andersons and Pachi stopped at Mariwazu, the Ticuna settlement near the Peruvian border. As they visited a house secluded from the others, they found only an old man. Lambert climbed the steps and with a smile greeted him "*Nuxmaxe*" (hello).

The man's jaw dropped as he stared at Lambert for long moments, then whispered: "Are you God?"

He had never seen a non-Ticuna Brazilian who spoke his language, much less a blond white man who could talk in the native tongue.

"No, I'm not God, but I've come to tell you about him," answered Lambert. "He is the One who made us, and he loves you. He sent his Son Jesus to earth so we can know him. If we believe in him we can be sure we will go to live with him forever. . . ."

"Could I hear more about him?" asked the aged man.

"Of course; come tonight to Quirino's house and we'll tell you more."

That night over a hundred Ticunas gathered to hear the Good News about Jesus Christ. After Pachi spoke, about twenty asked him to pray for them. They too wanted to follow the God who could give them life after death.

As they continued their journey upstream, Doris asked: "How can we share all the Lord has been doing on this trip? Why don't we call everyone in the village together and have Pachi give a report?" Lambert quickly seconded the idea.

Yaxya's wall-less house was one of the largest in the village, and all Cushillococha gathered there to hear about the downriver trip. Pachi reported in thrilling details how many of their brother Ticunas had placed their faith in Christ. "Wouldn't it be a shame," he concluded, "if the Lord should come and we who have heard so much about Christ were left behind, while so many of our people in other places would go to be with him because they have truly received him into their hearts?"

"Let's accept him right now," an outspoken one declared. And another: "We have heard for a long time and still continued in the old way." "Come, my wife and children, and you, too, my teen-age son over there," the Andersons heard. "Let's all accept him together."

The Indians gathered in family groups and prayed aloud for forgiveness of their sins. Tears glistened on their faces, and smiles broke out as God's peace overflowed their hearts. They were like brand new people—and the change went bone-deep. Practically the entire village of Cushillococha were now Christians . . . the Piro Indians had not prayed in vain!

"We need a bigger place to meet," said Jose that night. Everyone agreed that Alejandro's house was not large enough now. Now they needed a church building. "Our own church! Let's start building it right away."

The Ticunas decided on the site that evening and set up a committee to organize the work. The next day almost everyone was on the scene to start clearing away the forest in preparation for the construction of their meeting house.

One group was sent out to get posts, another to bring strong, straight poles for the framework. A third group collected bundles of leaves to weave into a thatch roof, and still another gathered vines to tie everything together. Soon the hardwood posts were set in place; the poles were tied and the framework was made for the roof.

Uchu, a former witchdoctor, was straddling the peak of the roof directing the others as Lambert came by one morning to express admiration. The woven palm-thatch roof was finished in about a week.

At Sunday school in the Anderson's house that week the people were keenly interested in the story of Solomon's new temple and the large picture illustrating it. "Our meeting house will be the most beautiful building in the village," the Indians decided with new inspiration.

Few Ticunas make walls for their house, but "God's house" must have walls. They decided on the best quality chestnut-colored hewn palm slabs to enclose the building.

Pretty Girl's father had an artistic bent, and he designed window strips which were strongly suggestive of the pointed arches he had seen on some faraway church. And Yaxya proudly presented a pulpit made of very light-colored wood which was adorned with a deep chestnut-colored cross.

In the midst of the building project in Cushillococha, the

Ticunas were honored by the visit of Dr. Efrain Morote Best, the Peruvian coordinator of jungle education. He was taking a survey of the Amazon River area to find out how the Peruvian Government could best aid the Indians.

Dr. Morote had an Indian background, and he was proud of his heritage. Once he had told a group of Indians from a number of jungle tribes: "When I ask some of you where you are from, I get the answer, 'from Lima,' or else, 'from Chosica' (which is close to Lima). Nobody wants to say that he is a jungle Indian, but I want to tell you brothers, I'm an Indian. When I first started school, I had to learn Spanish as a second language. Today when I think deeply about something I always think in my own language. Brothers, I'm an Indian. To have two languages is like having two heads: you have double ability!"

In the jungle village of Lake Cushillococha Dr. Morote observed the Ticunas working as a team to build their new church and he was impressed. He asked if they could be gathered so he could speak to them.

Assembled at Alejandro's house, the Ticunas listened closely. He had the ability to instill appreciation for the natives' unique language and culture. He opened the meeting by saying, "First of all, I have noted that here is a village where everyone speaks Ticuna! How would you like to have a school where you can learn to read and write in your own language? You can have teachers from your own tribe."

The Ticunas answered with applause, astonishment, and pleasure on their faces. It sounded like an incredible offer.

Lambert and Doris thought immediately of Uncle Cam's dream that a school system would be set up to enable all the tribes to become literate in their own language and also in Spanish. The minister of education in Peru had suggested this to Dr. Townsend in 1952, and the bilingual school system was born as a joint project of the ministry of education and the Summer Institute of Linguistics. In 1953 the first training course for Indian teachers was held in Yarinacocha with twelve tribal leaders from five tribes. This dream and plan were to leap ahead until 1974 would mark three hundred and thirty teachers training ten thousand Indian students in twenty-two languages and two hundred communities. That out did Uncle Cam's dream!

That memorable night in Cushillococha, Dr. Morote also spoke about the ownership of land. "How would you like to have titles to the land surrounding Cushillococha?"

They were speechless. In Peru the Indians never had land of their own. During the Spanish occupation, Indians and the land they occupied were the property of the Spanish patron. Even in the jungle, the Indians were told by merchants that all their produce must be sold to them. No one contested this monopolistic control. "What do you say? Would you like the official documents so you can call this your land?" repeated the Peruvian official.

The Ticunas dared to believe the "miracle" and clapped their approval. True to his word, Dr. Morote made the necessary contacts with the ministry of agriculture in Iquitos and within a month he was back with a land surveyor whom the Ticunas paid at 20 sols per household to plot their property.

On November 6, 1957, the minister of agriculture in Lima signed the final decree deeding some four thousand acres to the Ticuna Indians. Ever since, November 6 has been Independence Day in Cushillococha. Possessing their own land means they no longer need to hire themselves out to labor. They can sell their crops to anyone they choose and have become in a large measure economically independent.

The exhilaration of having their own land and school stirred the Ticunas to demonstrate their gratitude. "We don't have money, but we give our time and strength!" they vowed. They determined to make Cushillococha into a model village with streets flanked by new houses, and with a town plaza, a ball park, stores, and the school in addition to the new church just completed. Families strung out along the lake would move into new homes in the village so their children would not have to paddle long distances to school.

Constructing a new village was a multi-year task, but it mobilized the residents immediately. Underbrush had to be cut down, trees felled, and stumps removed. Men, women, and children attacked the jungle with machetes, axes, and bare hands.

The village plaza was laid out and streets were designed to follow the best contours of the land. Huge tree trunks had to be sawed into short lengths so that they could be rolled off the central area and burned along with the brush and stumps. In the center of the plaza a large ant mound covering several hundred square feet had to be removed. With no bulldozer to remove the dirt, Indians carried it away in baskets on their backs.

The new school was staked out to overlook the plaza which in turn bordered the lake. Jungle materials were brought for the construction, and the ironwood posts had been set by the time Lambert and Doris were scheduled to return to Yarinacocha for consolidation of their language progress.

Pachi and Jose accompanied the Andersons so they could attend school to become teachers. Pachi continued to help Lambert in the complicated analysis of the Ticuna language, and Doris began the long-term project of preparing primers to teach reading in both Ticuna and Spanish. Long lists of words and conversations had to be processed to determine which vowels, consonants, and syllable patterns were most frequent. Then, following the "Psycho-Phonemic Method" designed by Dr. Townsend, materials were organized so children could learn to read simple words in the first weeks of school.

Shortly after Pachi and Jose earned their teacher credentials, Lambert and Bob Wacker packed school materials and set out by truck with the teachers toward Pucallpa. There the teachers and supplies transferred to a boat bound for Iquitos while Bob and Lambert flew ahead to contract a large dugout to take them all to Cushillococha.

After three long days on the Amazon, the travelers reached the beautiful lake as a clear moon arched above. As they rounded the bend and approached the village, the new school loomed into view. "There it is! Look at it!" exclaimed Lambert. Standing straight in the center of the clearing, it invited students to the first day of school.

The next morning revealed extensive progress in the new village. The jungle had been peeled farther back to give place to the tiny model town of about three hundred people. The school playground area was cleared and a tall, straight flag pole soared upward in front of the school.

"*Atencion!*" commanded Pachi as fifty-eight children lined up for the first session. Jose hoisted the resplendent red and white national flag of Peru to the top of the pole, then the official enameled *escudo* (shield) was hung above the door as the school was inaugurated.

The gathered adults understood the importance of the day. "Our children won't be like us; now they'll be able to understand numbers and deal intelligently with the merchants. They'll know when the store keepers don't give the right weight or make the correct change."

"*Tutu, aru, tara, ucu. . . .*" It was the beginning of Ticuna children learning to read.

Merchants soon took note of what was happening. "I know all about Cushillococha!" a rum peddler was overheard. "I never go there anymore because I know it's no use. Nobody will buy, so I don't waste my time stopping there."

Christian Cushillococha had no more drunken fiestas, and Ticunas selling their products in Caballococha resolutely replied, "No, thank you" when offered rum by bargainers hoping to "soften them up" for advantageous deals.

"You think you're going to become angels now?" one taunted the Ticunas. "You're going to take wings and fly away? Well, come back to earth—here, have some rum." But the Indians were adamant.

Lambert learned that the town witchdoctor had died. He had been opposing the building of the village recently and Lambert wondered how to cope with treachery if it came. But Moreno was gone.

"Old Americo from the village downstream got sick and died," the Ticunas related. "His sons consulted another witchdoctor and heard that Moreno had hexed their father, so they invited him to a drinking party and after getting him drunk they gave him *masato* (yucca drink) mixed with ground glass. He was vomiting blood by the time he got home and he died four hours later."

Evil was still taking its toll, but Cushillococha was learning that the gift of God is life. Lambert and Doris could not find adequate words to praise God as they took leave of the Ticunas and returned to the United States with Betsy and Bert after five and a half years in Peru.

The change of environment was a bit traumatic for the children. Betsy had to be ordered by her parents to speak English to them—and their North American relatives. In moments of excitement Betsy reverted to her "native tongue," and in Lima when she was asked by Mrs. Cudney, the Institute house manager, to say something in the Indian language, Betsy told her mother in *Ticuna*: "Tell her I'm too small to talk Ticuna."

In Wisconsin the missionary family attended a wedding, and one of the memorable sidelights was Betsy's loud whisper: "Grandma, there's not a single bare foot here."

The year in the States brimmed with new adventures for the children, and Lambert and Doris had the privilege of informing Christian friends of the greatness of God toward the Ticunas.

Meduchu. *"I was just angry for no reason at all."* He is now studying in adult school because he wants to read God's Word for himself.

Chapter Ten "MAGNIFICO!"

"You wouldn't recognize Cushillococha! The area behind our back yard is full of houses and they're building more. Ten new families have arrived from downstream—they want to hear more of 'God's Word.'"

Lambert wrote the exciting news to Doris when he preceded her to their jungle home at the end of their year-long furlough in 1959. The school was thriving and the townspeople were enthusiastic. The main lake-front street was lined with many newly built houses. Even the Spanish-speaking people of the district capital, Caballococha, showed new respect for the Ticunas in Cushillococha.

Another change was at the school: Jose had resigned from teaching responsibilities and a new young man, Leonardo, had taken his place. Leonardo had married Lilia and he came to an understanding faith in Christ through Bob and Marion Wacker who substituted for the Andersons a part of the year. Leonardo had already completed the bilingual training course in Yarinacocha.

Back with the Ticunas together, the Andersons began their first substantial Bible translation: the book of Mark. They had successfully structured the basic pattern of the language so they could begin to write God's message in Ticuna style. This meant the shaping of hard and simpler texts in regular sequence rather than working with scattered easy passages.

At times it was a baffling struggle to wrest the thought from English or Spanish idiom into accurate Ticuna idiom. Pachi was still a competent helper, and he often supplied the right thought when Lambert was stuck. Mark 1:3 was difficult at first. "How would you say 'wilderness'?" queried Lambert. The Ticunas know about lush jungle, but nothing about desert. Pachi and Lambert finally agreed a good equivalent would be, "place where no one lives —uninhabited area."

Phrase by phrase, verse by verse, progress moved them through complicated passages and concepts foreign to the Ticunas. It would be a long time before the entire book was ready to print and there would be many checkings and recheckings, but the real translation venture was under-way.

This year was notable to the Andersons for another reason: Carl Cameron joined the family in Yarinacocha on July 4—a "real firecracker," some joked, and the fulfill-ment of the Piro Indian's prayer that God would give the bereaved Andersons two sons.

The Anderson children became endeared to the Ticunas as they grew up knowing and loving them and speaking the native language. The children became ardent observers of Ticuna culture—and sometimes mimics.

The children spent many hours in the Indian homes and never tired of playing in the Indian fires. One day a laugh-ing neighbor came over, hardly able to talk through his merriment as he described what had happened to four-year-old Bert. The youngster had put a tiny lemon into burning embers and it exploded, sending a shower of tiny coals in all directions. One of them landed in Bert's "cow-boot," and the Indian said he never saw such a dance until Bert's boot finally flew into the air and he sat down to rub his "hotfoot."

With the remarkable development of Cushillococha into a model village, Lambert began taking pictures and pre-pared an album of descriptive photos. They showed the neat streets, new houses, the church, the school, and also the newly installed bell of Cushillococha. Erected between sturdy jungle poles, it had become the heartbeat of the village, summoning the people to school, church, and any important gathering—a symbol of their new social structure and spiritual vitality. He also took numerous snapshots of the public work day activities as Ticunas worked soberly and happily together. "Lambert," said the Institute's director at Yarinacocha one day, "you should show this Ticuna album sometime to the national director of primary education, Dr. Luis Lopez Galarreta. We are under his jurisdiction in Indian education."

In Lima on vacation in 1960, Lambert had the album with him and he went to the office of Dr. Lopez and requested an interview. He was granted an appointment for the next day.

Shortly before the set time, Lambert arrived at the office to find the waiting room lined with people. Lambert looked at the crowd in dismay, but decided to approach the reception desk. The secretary noted his appointment and asked him to accompany her to the elevator. In moments they were walking into a small library on the tenth floor: there sat Dr. Lopez working on documents, and Lambert was introduced to him.

"May I have a few minutes of your time, Dr. Lopez, to show you a little bit of what you are doing out in the jungle?"

Dr. Lopez responded with a smile of appreciation and a correction: "It's what you are doing!" He took the album and began turning the pages.

"These should have appropriate titles!" he said enthusiastically. Then he started jotting down possible captions for the pictures. "This is tremendous!" he exclaimed as he also started to make notes of scenes where more government help would benefit the Ticunas. "Type up these captions and bring the album back tomorrow," Dr. Lopez requested. "I'd like to take this to the director of the International Labor Organization. He'd be interested in this project."

After an hour's interview, Lambert left Dr. Lopez, knowing he had found a real friend who sincerely desired to help the Indians.

The next day Dr. Lopez took Lambert to see the director

of the I.L.O. After almost two hours of conversation about the Ticunas, the two officials decided to take the matter to the head of the Agricultural Bank of Peru, and he promised his backing. Lambert left the album with Dr. Lopez so he could interest others in the Ticunas and their needs.

In 1961, when Dr. Lopez became coordinator of the Ministry of Education, next in authority to the minister, he decided to publish a collection of basic books for all the nation's school libraries. Various themes were highlighted: the subject of demonstrating what a community could do to help itself and the country reminded Dr. Lopez of the progress in Cushillococha and he chose the Ticuna story as a national example. A well-known author was appointed to write the book and thirty thousand copies were printed to depict what could be accomplished by a group of people committed to working together. The book was illustrated by many of Lambert's pictures.

In the Ticuna village one afternoon, Jose, the recently elected mayor of Cushillococha, came to Lambert with a new idea. "We need to have electricity here." But the concept seemed impractical if not impossible.

But Jose was serious. He wanted electricity for the adult evening school which he hoped would begin soon. Kerosene lamps were so dim, even for the children doing their homework at night. Lambert didn't want to discourage Jose, but he did wonder how such a "miracle" could occur.

Some weeks later Lambert checked with an official from the district capital, Caballococha, and found that their light plant had been procured from the National Fund of Economic Development. Was this a lead?

That September as Lambert passed through Iquitos on his way to Yarinacocha base he remembered Jose's request. Knowing the governor of the state resided here, Lambert decided to see him. Finding that he was in conference, Lambert was presented instead to his wife who was passing through the hall. She suggested that he return late that afternoon when her husband would be available. As Lambert went by the guard at the door, he was quietly informed, "You know the governor's wife is a North American, don't you?"

Returning that afternoon, Lambert found both the governor and his wife at his headquarters. "Did you realize that you made me use my best Spanish this morning?" Lambert asked her in English. They all laughed. The governor's wife, Senora Morla Concha, was from Newton, Kansas, and had met him while he was a Peruvian army representative in Washington, D.C. The governor was very encouraging to Lambert and gave him a letter of introduction to the secretary general of the National Fund.

Lambert followed through by going to the president of the board of public works of the State of Loreto with a written request asking that he include a light plant for the Ticuna Village in the budget of 1962. At least the first steps had been taken and Jose could hope for results.

At Yarinacocha Lambert and Pachi delved deeper into the translation of Mark. The fascinating narrative of miracles and the parables, the character description of Jesus Christ, and God's unfolding plan in the cross captivated their minds and souls, and they made good progress.

One day the party-line phone rang in the little study where Lambert and Pachi were working. The Institute director wanted Lambert to come to his office. There he asked Lambert to travel to Lima to attend to an urgent matter of mission business. "I'd prefer to stay," was Lambert's reply. "We're really making good progress on the translation work and I'd rather not go right now." But the director's sense of urgency finally persuaded Lambert to assume the responsibility.

While in Lima Lambert decided to vist Dr. Lopez and mention the Ticunas' desire for a lighting plant. By now Dr. Lopez himself had visited Cushillococha, and when he heard about the electric project, he decided to write a letter for Lambert to take with a copy of the book, *Pueblo Ticuna,* to the secretary general of the National Fund for Economic Development. Lambert was able to arrange an appointment the day before he would be returning to Yarinacocha.

The morning of the appointment, Lambert had an errand near the office of the Secretary General, but he was an hour early. The Institute office was some distance away, and Lambert decided to chance seeing the official early.

"The Secretary General is free just at this moment," the receptionist advised Lambert. And within minutes Lambert was ushered in. "As soon as I've finished with Mr. Anderson," the executive told his secretary, "send in the president and his board of works for Loreto."

Lambert stared in amazement. "Mr. Secretary General—I'm from the State of Loreto, and the matter I've come to discuss concerns a project to be presented by them."

The Secretary General then asked his receptionist to send in the waiting committee, and he turned to the letter from Dr. Lopez. He had read most of it before the Loreto delegation arrived, and after cordial greetings were exchanged he said, "Gentlemen, please be seated, I want to read a letter to you." He then read the entire letter from Dr. Lopez. Addressing the head of the board, he asked, "Mr. President, what do you plan to do for the Ticunas this year?"

"Mr. Secretary General," came the reply, "we have considered possibilities, but have nothing definite as yet. We are really short on funds."

The officer continued: "Gentlemen, if I would give this light plant to the Ticunas this year, would you be willing to include it in your budget for the next year?"

Lambert would never forget the response: "Magnifico!" And the transaction was completed. Letters were prepared to Dr. Lopez and to Jose, the mayor of Cushillococha. Electric lights would soon shine in Ticuna jungle homes!

In June of 1962, a 20-kilowatt, diesel-powered electric plant of the highest quality in Lima was purchased for the

Ticunas. Also included were the wire and electrical supplies needed to install lighting along the streets.

The Indians set to work to make everything ready for the arrival of the equipment. For light poles, they hewed out thirty-foot hardwood posts that were so heavy a dozen men had to carry each one. More than fifty of these poles were needed.

They ordered cement from Iquitos and brought sand from the Amazon River banks to make the floor of the light plant building and base for the generator. Boards for the walls of the twenty-by-twenty building were sawed by hand from a single large tree. Corrugated metal roofing was purchased, and soon the building was ready for the machinery which arrived late one afternoon on a Peruvian Army boat. The Army even sent a technician to install the generator. It didn't take long until all was completed—the engine, control panel, lines, and lights on the poles for street lighting in the village.

November 17, 1962, dawned auspiciously for Cushillococha, only a week and a half following their Independence Day anniversary on November 6. This inauguration day of the electric light plant brought a planeload of officials from Lima, Iquitos, and Yarinacocha on the Catalina.

Ticunas lined the bank as the guests stepped off the planes and were welcomed by Jose and other village officials. Then everyone gathered at the light plant for the ceremony.

The Ticuna teachers and Doris had worked long hours training the boys and girls for their participation. They marched proudly and stood at rigid attention before the assembly, then as Leonardo gave the signal they broke out lustily in the national anthem of Peru. It didn't seem possible that these Indian children had never held a pencil such a short time before. The visitors nodded with approval and applauded spontaneously as the children recited patriotic poems memorized for the occasion.

Then Pachi, the first school teacher, stepped forward and

addressed the gathering. "Today, a day of culmination for an Indian village of the Amazon jungle of our beloved Peru, I have the honor of welcoming you to Cushillococha. I say 'day of culmination' because truly, in a deep sense, this day represents for me, as well as for you, my brothers of this village, the culmination of a living miracle.

"You are in the land inhabited for centuries by my ancestors. Oh, that it were possible for them to be here for this occasion of which they couldn't even dream in those days in which they lived as shadows in the forest and then as servants of the exploiters of wild rubber! From being 'owners' of the jungle, they became dominated by those who had the advantages of civilization and an education. They lost their 'nobility' to become servants."

Pachi went on to tell how their inheritance had been continual insecurity, and in those circumstances Dr. Morote had arrived to help them. Then he listed the achievements gained since that time. He concluded his remarks by saying:

"Distinguished visitors, we consider that the success of Cushillococha was made possible not just through the efforts of its people, nor just through the efforts of our government, but through a collaboration of the two. In our country we have always desired the best for our *families* and we believe that now our children will have a much more prosperous future than that which was ours. By placing all our efforts at the disposition of our *country*, we have received a recompense much greater than that which we could ever expect. Finally, we want to serve *God*. Before we each went our own way, but in recent years we've had the privilege of knowing our God and his commandments, through his Holy Word. From being, as the Bible says, 'lost sheep,' we have put our faith and complete confidence in him. And he, beyond giving us eternal life, has blessed us much more in this world than a simple village of Indians could ever expect. Day after day he has given us light in our souls and now, a new light for our village as well. We can do no less than to give him all of our thanks.

"Distinguished visitors, we want to serve to the best of our abilities, our families, our country, and our God. It is our sacred duty."

Following Pachi, Uncle Cam spoke. He reminded the Ticunas of his previous visit eight years before and of his dreams for them since that time. Now his happiness was complete to be present for this special event and to see the way God had blessed them as they had put their faith in him and had followed his Word.

Then came the climax of the ceremony—turning on the lights. The key to start the generator was turned by engineer Ernesto Noriega Calmet, director of public lands for the jungle, who had prepared the documents that deeded the land to the Ticunas. Dr. Lopez, their friend from Lima, pushed the starter. He had been given the academic push to get the Ticunas going in education. Next came the throwing of the light switches by the mayor of Iquitos and president of the public works board of the State of Loreto, and a Peruvian friend, Miss Rosita Corpancho, who had helped arrange the procurement of the light plant.

Shadowed Cushillococha flared into a shining oasis, a sparkling necklace glimmering in the waters of the jungle lake. A spectacular evening! Conversation in Ticuna and Spanish buzzed on into the night hours with the exhilaration of it all. The Ticunas overflowed with ideas of new progress.

For the twenty-eight guests, it was an unforgettable outing. The table was loaded with a variety of jungle food as well as delights brought from Yarinacocha by Elaine Townsend. In the late hours everyone found some place to sleep: on bunks in the Catalina; in sleeping bags in the carpenter shop, the translation study, and the living room; and Uncle Cam crawled under the kitchen table where his air mattress fit snugly.

At breakfast the next morning with everyone gathered around the table, Uncle Cam took his New Testament from his shirt pocket and read from chapter ten of the Gospel of John—the story of the Good Shepherd.

Then the Mayor of Iquitos spoke of the value of the Bible to him. "I wrote my doctor's thesis on the Book of Romans," he said. "I had taken my Grandmother's Bible with me to the university. One day a fire broke out and swept through the locker room building. It came right to where the Bible lay, and there it stopped." To him, he added, the Bible had always been the substance of enduring truth. Others added personal experiences and observations.

It was Sunday, and many of the guests were present as the Ticunas worshiped together and gave thanks to God for what he had done.

Shortly before the visitors were to leave, the director of education from Iquitos spoke with Lambert, "I have some funds available to build new schools in this area. I'd like to help the Ticunas by providing a permanent structure with board walls and floor and a corrugated metal roof that won't require continual changing like the thatch."

The matter was discussed with the teachers who were elated with the news. Sometime later, a new twenty-by-sixty-five-foot school building was erected to take the place of the first school which was already needing repair. White with blue trim, the impressive structure looked like a palace to the Ticunas. The words of the Ticuna patriotic hymn rang true—"How beautiful is our school in Cushillococha!"

It was not long before the first of the New Testament books was translated. Many months had been spent to find suitable equivalents for such words as *angel, baptism, bless, condemn, disciple, hell, heaven, holy, judgment, parable, Passover, sacrifice, prophet, scribe, spirit,* and *witness.* Months of checking and rechecking would be necessary before the Institute was satisfied the manuscript was ready for printing.

As the Andersons struggled with the complications of the Ticuna language, they became increasingly concerned about helping others follow their steps, such as the missionaries working with Ticunas in Brazil. As a result, Doris started work on a series of practical lessons based on Lambert's technical analysis of the grammar. Included were dialogues, drills, and explanatory information needed for a basic grasp of Ticuna. The final product was a four-hundred page textbook called *Conversational Ticuna* which was published in Yarinacocha. It was demanding enough for Doris to label it her "Life and Works."

By 1964 it was time for furlough. Ten years in Ticuna-land had produced much fruit, yet much seed had not sprouted. The Book of Mark was available for reading in the Ticuna school program, but twenty-six new Testament books remained untranslated!

Traveling to the U.S. with three children was a new and unpredictable experience for the missionaries. Not long after their plane landed in Florida, the boys were excitedly discussing the wonders around them when Cam silenced everyone with the loud rebuke: "No, Bert; it's not your Ami. It's my Ami."

In Wisconsin Grandma had a big cake flying American flags for Cam's fifth birthday. That night he also attended the local Fourth of July celebration where he caught fragments from an American flag stretched across the sky by spectacular fireworks.

There were so many friends and churches to visit where the three children were encouraged to be on their best behavior. One evening in a church fellowship time the two Anderson boys hurried across the basement room to their parents, and conversation paused sufficiently for the crowd to hear: "Mommy, we just found the Baptists' tub! Come see—it's upstairs behind the curtain!"

As the weather turned cold and the family journeyed to Wheaton College in Illinois for further "adult education," the children asked repeatedly: "Why do people stay here?" Cam and Bert couldn't wait to get back to the hot jungle.

Lambert and Doris spent a profitable school year taking Spanish and Latin American studies in finishing work for advanced degrees. The classes in history and literature were especially interesting after the years of living in Peru. Doris also learned how to use the laundromat once a week, serve meals on paper plates, and keep house while taking a normal study schedule. Lambert carried school work with him as he spent weekends telling church congregations of God's blessings among the Ticunas.

And suddenly it was August 1965, and the Ticuna expatriates were ready to return to Peru.

Cuere's wife weaving a "yucca squeezer," used to extract moisture from the grated yucca prior to toasting. (Don Hesse)

Chapter Eleven **HANDCRAFTED**

Lambert listened in awe from the back of the Ticuna church. A year before he had sat in this very spot listening to messages from God's Word in Ticuna by another Indian leader. Who had appointed the school teacher, Leonardo? And where did he get the burning message that kept his audience on the edge of their benches?

"A man before God is like a dugout canoe. You don't chop down just any tree in the forest to make one—you can look for days before you find the right timber. After you fell the tree you cut it the right length and hew it, little by little, so it will be exactly uniform. Then you gouge out the inside, gauging carefully the depth as you go along. You might chisel for days and maybe even weeks or months to reach the exact thickness you want."

Lambert knew the canoes were a work of craftsmanship as well as means of transport. Dugouts conveyed Ticunas to faraway relatives, and no customized-car owner in Detroit is prouder of his vehicle than a Ticuna who travels in a perfectly crafted canoe he has built.

"After you soak the shell of your new canoe for the proper time, you slowly 'open' the sides over a fire so it will be flat and stable. After the canoe has cooled you painstakingly go over every square inch of the inside with your sharp hand adz to make a perfectly finished interior. You plane red cedar for the benches, and at last your canoe is just what you wanted it to be—a work of art.

"Likewise," said the pastor to his full congregation,

"God works on us to create exactly what he wants us to be. We don't become perfect Christians in one day—it takes a long time for God to shape us and mold us. But day after day as he labors over us he's looking forward to that time he has planned when our lives will be splendid examples of Christ."

Not that day nor the next but much later Lambert learned the thrilling story behind Leonardo's long ascent to the spiritual leadership among the Ticunas.

■ ■ ■ ■

". . . C'mon! Get up, Leonardo! What are you doing in bed? It's already after 3 A.M. and there's no firewood and not a drop of water in the jugs. How can I start to cook for the day?" The house girl shook the tired Indian boy as she scolded him.

He'd have to hurry now to get all the chores done before school started. "Why did the teacher seem to make an example of an Indian boy to teach the Mestizos not to be tardy?" Leonardo wondered groggily. The Spanish-speaking boys always snickered at the Indians' failures. Naturally, the majority were superior, and Indians were the ridiculed minority in the Spanish-speaking school at Caballococho.

Leonardo was born downriver in Cushillococha in 1940, and when he was only four years old his family moved upstream to the Yacarate River where his father worked rubber trees. With no bilingual schools, Indian parents with high goals for their sons had to send them to a Spanish-speaking school where they bore the brunt of jokes by monolingual Mestizo students.

Leonardo earned part of his keep in the merchant's home by carrying in firewood and jugs of water from before daybreak until school started. He washed his own clothes, and sometimes went to school hungry because there had been no time to eat. Life was not easy, but Leonardo was determined not to disappoint his father and at seventeen years of age he successfully completed his studies.

Leonardo's father was proud of his educated son, but there was still manual labor to be done. The boy accompanied his father daily on dawn-to-sunset walks collecting latex sap from little tins attached to rubber trees. How his eyes burned in the evening as he dripped the fresh latex over the ball shaped around the pole his father turned in the smoking shed! But it would bring a good price if they could find an honest merchant. Then they could buy cloth and soap and maybe even a shotgun. And now in three months he would be going back to Cushillococha to marry Lilia who had been promised to him when he had last visited his relatives there.

The anticipated time came and Leonardo returned to Cushillococha to move into Lilia's home. Sharing the same mosquito net was the official marriage ceremony of the Indian culture. The proximity of her parents is a reassurance to the new bride that she will not be mistreated.

"Let's go to hear God's Word," Lilia suggested to her husband a few days after their marriage.

"That doesn't interest me," Leonardo demurred. "I'd rather lie in my hammock and play the ukulele." Several weeks of Lilia's gentle entreaties followed and one Sunday Leonardo agreed: "All right; I'll go this time and see for myself."

Leonardo couldn't believe what he heard. Pachi was saying God wants the Indians to live for him? How could he care about someone as insignificant as Leonardo? The Ticunas considered him educated, but he didn't know anything compared to the merchants.

"Jesus died for me? That can't be. I wasn't even born then. That sounds like some notion the White Man's given to Pachi, but he's reading right from the Bible and the teacher in school said that's a true book. Does it really say those things about me? I do like that idea of God caring about me."

After the meeting Leonardo told Lilia, "I'm going to come with you again. This sounds interesting!"

It was the summer of 1958 and the Andersons were on furlough. Bob Wacker and his wife, Marion, had to spend their vacation in Cushillococha with their four children. "We should learn as much of the language as we can while we're here," Bob determined. As Pachi was busy teaching in the school and was leading the Sunday meetings, Bob looked elsewhere for a language helper and saw Leonardo as a bright possibility.

But teaching his language to a white man was quite different from struggling to learn Spanish, Leonardo found. Could his language really be that difficult? Fortunately, they could communicate fairly easily in Spanish. Their discussions veered naturally to God, and one day as they talked together Leonardo opened his heart to the Savior. Now he and Lilia were united spiritually as well as in marriage.

When the Wackers returned to Yarinacocha, Bob suggested that Leonardo enter the teacher training course along with Pachi. That was the beginning of a teaching career that would elevate him in 1974 to the post of supervisor for all the bilingual schools in various villages. And in Caballococha Leonardo would meet a former Mestizo school mate and hear him say:

"I used to laugh at you in school, Leonardo, because I thought you were my inferior. Now I see that I have nothing but drunkenness while you have nice clothes and shoes and a clean life. Keep on following God like you're doing—now you're really my superior!"

Leonardo's teaching ability surfaced quickly. One day shortly after the Andersons' return from their first furlough, Lambert took a guest to visit a math class. In ten minutes Leonardo glided through varied illustrations of addition. "How many marks are there on the blackboard? And how many are these? How many fingers are these? And how many on this hand? And how many all together?

You two, stand up! And you and you and you! How many are these? And how many all together? These sticks, how many. . . ?"

The astonished guest turned to Lambert and commented, "Don't let that young man loose in New York—he'd be mayor of the city in five years!"

Soon after the installation of the light plant, the state supervisor of education was visiting on Callaru River, thirty miles downstream from Cushillococha. He found many Ticuna families scattered for miles along the river, and in his report he suggested a bilingual school be opened in the area. Leonardo and another young teacher were chosen to contact the people and gather them together to start a school.

The job wasn't simple. "Why should we leave our present homes?" objected the Ticunas. "Who sent you to talk to us? Will our children really learn in the school you're proposing?" But with Leonardo's characteristic enthusiasm nudging them on, the Indians selected a suitable area and started to clear jungle growth to construct a "little Cushillococha."

When Lambert first visited the area, there was already a clearing. Posts stood in place for the new school and leaves were being woven to form the roof.

A year later Lambert returned to find a rapidly developing village. A soccer field overlooking the river was bordered on three sides by straight streets and sixteen new homes. And on the front edge of the soccer field stood the new school, with a red and white flag waving in the breeze. They named the new village "Bellavista" (Beautiful View), and Lambert's heart saw much more than an attractive community.

By this time Gospel Recordings, Inc., of Los Angeles had come to the Ticunas and made tapes of Pachi and Leonardo speaking and of a group of Ticunas singing. And an excellent set of eight teaching records came back to aid in evangelistic trips to outlying Ticuna villages.

"Imagine that black plate talking our language, and even singing in our language about God!" exclaimed the Indians. "Does God know our language? Listen, it talks about life that never ends! Play it again."

The records reached many isolated villages which the missionary did not have opportunity to visit, and time after time the response to them was "Play them again!" And as they listened Indian hearts were gradually changed.

Cuere was another Ticuna that God laid his hand upon. Years before the Andersons' coming to Peru, Cuere had been sentenced to prison for murder. At a drunken fiesta when he was only fifteen, Cuere got in a fight with his brother-in-law Chaiye. Under the effects of liquor, Chaiye had pulled out his long hunting knife and menacingly asked Cuere, "How would you like to feel the edge of this?" Cuere went to his traveling bag and pulled out his own knife. The two were squaring off when a third man picked up a club to hit Cuere. As the man swung, Cuere flailed out in self-defense and his knife went through the man's heart. The next day policeman arrived to take Cuere to the district jail from which he was sent to Iquitos for sentencing and the long term of imprisonment. Only a presidential pardon brought his release.

Returning to Cushillococha after six years in prison was like beginning life all over again. It was also the first time for Cuere to hear God's Word and he soon became an earnest Christian.

Several years later on a Sunday morning, Cuere heard a message from Mark 16:15—"Go ye into all the world and preach the gospel to every creature." The speaker closed by asking who would be willing to go from Cushillococha with the gospel to other Ticunas. One hand was raised: Cuere's.

It was no idle commitment. Missionaries from the Swiss Indian Mission had set up a Bible school for jungle Indians near Pucallpa, and Cuere enrolled. He became one of the first graduates, wanting to serve the Lord above all. The

Ticunas of Cushillococha recognized his deep desire and made him their pastor as well as a traveling missionary.

In the summer of 1964 while the Andersons were on furlough, Cuere encountered new trouble. He was asked by local authorities to be constable in charge of keeping peace in the village, and a serious problem with a witchdoctor arose.

Macawachi lived upstream from Cushillococha, but his success in treating dying Indians gained him fame in the Christian village. But Macawachi liked liquor, and one afternoon while drunk he created a loud disturbance which Cuere, the constable, tried to quell. His intervention caused the witchdoctor to fly into a rage and then he turned and walked away. That night Cuere's ten-year-old son fell ill and in two days he died.

Macawachi's conduct became steadily worse. When he was drunk he bragged about his occult powers, and many claimed he put secret hexes on people and then charged a fee to make them well. Turmoil over Macawachi increased until some of the Ticunas reported it to district authorities and Macawachi was ordered to leave Cushillococha or face arrest.

On the eve of his departure Macawachi got drunk and threatened to hex the entire village. On the pretext of getting fish for his journey, several men reportedly invited Macawachi to go fishing at the upper end of the lake—but the witchdoctor never returned from the fishing trip. Because Cuere's son had died suddenly, Cuere was among those who were questioned by the police. The stigma made it impossible for Cuere to continue in his pastoral position, though his Christian service did not end.

Meanwhile, in this crisis of leadership, God began working in Leonardo's heart to prepare him for new responsibilities.

Lucas helps his people with their medical needs. Recently, using vaccine supplied by the Ministry of Public Health, 487 children were vaccinated when an epidemic of measles threatened to sweep the Ticuna villages of Cushillococha, Bellavista, and Bufeococha. (Leo Lance)

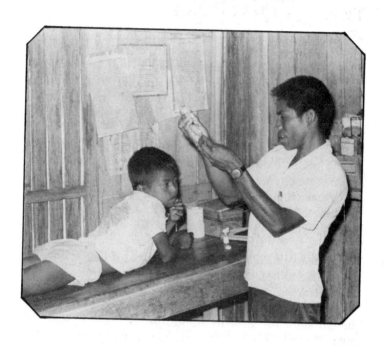

Chapter Twelve **MIRACLE**

The veiled moon disappeared behind thickening clouds as the wooden-hulled river boat chugged up the Amazon. The kerosene lantern that swung above the pilot's cabin was incapable of lighting the way; it only warned other boats that might be navigating through the backwaters close to the towering walls of trees and vines. Small boats traveling upstream always keep close to the bank rather than battle the swift current that churns down the middle of the river. The boat had left Caballococha three days before and another three days would be required to reach Iquitos.

Under the roof of the open boat weary passengers swung in a haphazard array of hammocks. Tired grumbles merged with slaps at ever-present mosquitos. Everyone had wished the trip were over soon after it started, and by now the strain of travel was telling on everyone.

"Leonardo, her fever seems worse." In the maze of hammocks toward the back of the boat, the Ticuna man reached out his hand and felt the forehead of his two-year-old daughter, but said nothing. What can you say when your little girl gets steadily more listless and there's nothing you can do?

They had tried to get reservations on the pontoon plane that made the flight each week, but somehow they were always last on the list. As a last resort, Leonardo and Lilia got passage on the *Yacupato* for the six-day trip.

As the boat labored toward the dim lights of Pebas, the next village ahead, Lilia's anxiety became increasingly evident. Leonardo's brain began running through every possibility for help—look for a doctor or at least a medical post . . . ask if there's a radio to call for help . . . rent a speed boat—"Dear Lord, will you help an Indian!"

Two and a half hours after a glancing collision with a floating log, the boat tied up in a makeshift port created by high water conditions. Half a dozen sleepy villagers stumbled through the dark to see if there was anything special for sale. They drifted back to their homes and Leonardo returned to tossing in his hammock waiting for the first glow in the east.

Leonardo was jerked awake at dawn as his wife shook the hammock. "Leonardo, you have to do something. People must be up by now—at least try to find some store that has 'Mejoral' aspirin to cool the fever."

The village was at the top of the hill and Leonardo found several stores—all closed. At the last door he decided to knock anyway.

A small shutter flew open. "Who are you, anyway, and what are you trying to do? Anyone with sense doesn't wake people before the sun is up!"

"But Senor, my daughter has a terrible fever. Don't you have some Mejoral? I have money and I'll pay for it no matter what it costs."

"I have Mejoral but the store isn't open yet. Come back at a civil hour, eight o'clock, and I'll take care of you!"

When Leonardo got back to the boat his distraught wife reproached him for taking so long when their child's life was at stake. Leonardo faced a critical decision: either he had to get other transportation or resign himself to three more days and nights of river travel and possibly the death of their daughter enroute. There was only one choice; he raced back up the hill to the village.

After asking several people he learned of a village with a small speed boat which had been rented on several occasions. Inquiring still further, he found his way to the mud-walled house where the man was just finishing breakfast.

"Senor, my name is Leonardo Witancort and I'm a 'maestro bilingue.' I teach in the school downstream in Cushillococha. My baby is terribly sick and I have to get her to a doctor before she dies. They tell me that you rent your boat and I'd like to know if I could rent it from you. I'll pay whatever you ask."

The man studied the inquirer. "How do I know you'll bring it back? What documents do you have?"

"Here is my 'carnet de maestro,' Senor."

The man took the document and studied it carefully —the back as well as the front. It was evident that it was official. Finally he replied, "How much money do you have?"

"I have twelve hundred sols with me, and I promise to take good care of the boat and motor."

The man knew a good deal when he saw it, and with a nod of assent he led the way down to the port where the boat and motor were kept.

The whistle on the *Yacupato* had already blown when Leonardo got back to tell his wife that God had helped him find a speed boat. Now it would be a trip of five hours instead of three days. Hurriedly they gathered their belongings and informed the captain they were traveling by other means.

The speed boat was a welcome change. Traveling at almost 20 mph they saw Pebas quickly disappear behind them as the broad expanse of the Amazon lay ahead. The Mejoral gave a temporary benefit but in the hot sun the baby's fever returned. Worse, she seemed to lie limp with no will to live. The motor was not running smoothly as they passed the mouth of the Ampiyaco River but they were still making fast time.

They had covered two-thirds of their journey when the motor stopped. Leonardo lifted the reserve gas tank he had connected a short time earlier and found it dry. A short distance back they had noticed a fiesta in progress, and they paddled downstream to search for gas. The party goers referred them to a merchant a bit further downstream who had a motor.

The merchant was amiable but he was unwilling to "sell" to someone without money.

"I'll give you my identification papers and when you come to Iquitos I'll redeem them from you," pleaded Leonardo.

The man agreed, and the refueled boat started upstream again. By this time it was late afternoon and the parents were anxious over the delay. Then, one-fourth the distance from Iquitos, the motor died again. This time the problem was not gasoline. Leonardo cleaned the sparkplugs, checked the wires, and pulled and pulled on the starter rope until he dropped with exhaustion. They were stranded and dusk was approaching. Their child seemed more dead than alive. What could they do? They looked to the Lord for help.

Leonardo had a Gospel of Mark and he thought of the ten crises in that book where Jesus met each one with a miracle. The book was filled with God's working among men. Leonardo and Lilia were sure that the Lord could meet their crisis also, and they believed he would.

Soon after they prayed, a large canoe powered by a Penta workhorse motor appeared. Leonardo hailed the boat and it turned toward the bank. The owner was willing to take Leonardo and his family but not the boat. But Leonardo could not abandon the boat and his pleading finally resulted in a reluctant agreement to tow them to Iquitos.

Darkness had fallen when the lights of Iquitos shimmered in ribbons across the dark river. Only after they had docked in a small outlying port did Leonardo dare to tell the owner that he had no money with him but he would get some from his friend in Iquitos immediately.

On the street above the river they hailed a taxi that took them to their friend's home. Don Bernardo gladly lent Leonardo the needed money.

Then, taking one look at the dehydrated child, he

realized the urgency of finding a doctor. After going from one office to another they located a doctor who administered several shots to try to cool the soaring temperature.

The next morning the child was as fever-ravaged as ever, and they took her back to the doctor who could only administer another shot. For days she had eaten nothing, and her emaciated body showed the toll taken by the unknown illness.

The following day was Sunday, and Don Bernardo suggested, "Why don't you bring your little girl to church tonight and we'll ask the pastor to pray for her? God can heal her."

Leonardo was at the end of his own resources; there were no other solutions. Rocked with weariness and tension, he answered, "I think that's what we should do."

That night after the service they came with Don Bernardo to make their special request. The pastor was frank: "Leonardo, do you believe God can heal your child?"

"Yes, yes, I know he can," was the quick reply.

"Then let's pray for her and ask that God will work a miracle this very night."

The tropical air was starting to cool as they left the church. A rustling breeze was blowing off the Amazon and black clouds hung in the sky.

Suddenly as they were driving home the child sat up and looked at Lilia. "Mom, I want bread," she asked. Her eyes were bright and snapping. God had answered their prayers! From that moment on the girl showed complete recovery.

That night Leonardo made a lifetime commitment to God. He wanted to serve this gracious Master with all of his energy.

■ ■ ■ ■

Lambert and Doris Anderson listened in wonder to the details of Leonardo's story. So this was the reason

Leonardo preached with such understanding and conviction. God had prepared him while they were away for a ministry that would change Cushillococha and reach Ticunas up and down the great jungle river.

Betsy with some of her tribal friends. Elena, left, is now in SIM Bible School with her husband, Calixto. (Eugene Loos)

Chapter Thirteen **LIMA**

The telephone call in the Institute's Lima office was for Senor Anderson. As he took the call, Lambert was surprised to hear a spokesman from the palace of President Belaunde. The conversation was brief and Lambert concluded it with: "I will be most honored to accept the invitation to dinner."

Being liaison man with the government for the Summer Institute of Linguistics during 1966 was full of pleasant surprises. Lambert was asked to take the Institute directorship upon his return from furlough, but he had accepted with some misgivings. Expecting unaccustomed pressures, he and Doris instead experienced rewarding opportunities.

The minister of public works and other government officials were among the guests at the palace dinner. Lambert talked to the president about the activities of the Institute's linguists and specifically of the progress among the Ticunas. "We live in the northeastern corner of the jungle near Caballococha," Lambert explained.

The president replied, "But don't you work in Cushillococha?" The president's acquaintance with the remote Indian village amazed Lambert, but it reflected the executive's extensive travel.

"And when is Dr. Townsend coming to Peru again?" the president inquired. Upon learning that he would be arriving in two months, the president instructed one of his aides to keep in touch with Lambert. When Uncle Cam returned to Lima, the president invited him to an official dinner as guest of honor. It was an impressive expression of goodwill for Townsend and his linguists.

As the year progressed, Lambert encountered many friends among the Peruvian officials. The Summer Institute of Linguistics participated jointly with the government in a bilingual teacher training program responsible for over one hundred teachers in seventy communities. Lambert and Doris realized the post in Lima proved to have as many challenges as they had faced in the jungle village.

A city of three million people on the Pacific Ocean, Lima seemed another world to the Andersons. But a strong link was maintained with their jungle village through Maria, their Indian house girl who kept them conversing in Ticuna. They lived in a separate apartment of the new, motel-style Group House in an area of moderately priced homes on Avenida Javier Prado, only six blocks from the seacoast.

The Group House hummed with hospitality and activity. Mrs. Cudney provided a homey atmosphere for friends visiting the city. A two-story wing of sixteen bedrooms, with a bath between each two rooms, furnished comfortable housing. Another section included the kitchen where Mrs. Cudney planned the delicious meals that were prepared by her capable staff to be served in a dining room accommodating sixty-five people. It was a refreshing retreat for translators who needed a break from the heat and testings of the jungle work.

The climate and surroundings were so different in Lima. Fog billowed in off the ocean and cooled the whole area during the hot months of December through April. The great variation from the wet jungle was the near-absence of rain. All the beautiful parks and gardens were greened by piped water.

Lambert and Doris found the political system of Peru a fascinating study. A republic, Peru was liberated from Spanish rule in 1821 by San Martin and Bolivar, the founding fathers. The country is divided into twenty-three states called "departments." Each department is composed of provinces which in turn are divided into districts. The smallest segment is the municipal agency, with an agent appointed by district council and answerable to the district mayor. Cushillococha qualified as an agency, and Jose was its first agent, later succeeded by Leonardo.

The biggest project for Lambert in Lima was the celebration of the Institute's twentieth anniversary in Peru. Rosita Corpancho worked long hours with him to plan the activities. Others in the office worked double time to compile a book of articles and pictures about the work in the tribes, and three thousand copies were printed. Rare artifacts and an authentic jungle hut were featured in a display at the famous exposition hall of the Banco Continental.

A series of lectures was held in the Casa de Cultura, one of Lima's historical conference halls, featuring the Institute's accomplishments in linguistics, anthropology, education, and community development. The discourses were given by outstanding educators of Peru including Dr. Carlos Cueto, the Minister of Education, who spoke the final night. These men were all deeply interested in the needs of their people in the jungle.

A special dinner in the Americas room of Hotel Bolivar, situated on the San Martin downtown plaza, was given in honor of Dr. Townsend. Friends and officials from all over Lima gathered to pay him homage. Lambert and Doris conversed in Ticuna for the guests to hear a tonal language. Then Uncle Cam had a special request, "Doris, could you sing the Ticuna patriotic hymn?" The elaborate dining room with white-coated waiters and elegantly clothed guests seemed a strange setting for the song born in the jungle, but it carried a magic of its own.

The next day at the National University of San Marcos the president of the university, who also was president of the Senate of Peru, conferred an honorary doctorate of education upon William Cameron Townsend. Only six honorary doctorates had been granted in the four-hundred-year history of the National University—the sixth man had been General Charles de Gaulle. Explaining why the Summer Institute of Linguistics had come to Peru, Dr. Townsend said, "As in Mark 10 verse 45 it is recorded that the Son of Man came not to be served but to serve; so our linguists have come to Peru not for personal profit but to serve." He went on to describe how the Indians' ability to read and write in their own language formed a natural bridge to the national language and a more effective understanding of Spanish as well as the language of their own tribe.

A week later, a second celebration was held at the Yarinacocha base. An official party, including the Minister of Education and his family, arrived there just in time for Uncle Cam's birthday. Dr. Cueto witnessed examples of the translation work being done among twenty-four Indian tribes, and he received enthusiastic applause from the Shipibo Indians as he donned a native robe and crown they presented. Someone remarked that he was one of the tallest Shipibos they had ever seen—he was also tall in greatness as a friend of all the Indians.

Later the president of Peru visited Yarinacocha. He talked with the Indians studying in the occupational training courses and asked them about their different backgrounds. Then he visited the school grounds of the Institute children, some of them skilled in at least three languages—English, Spanish, and the idiom of the Indians with which their parents worked. Standing together to greet the president, the boys and girls sang the Peruvian national anthem for him. Lambert presented Betsy, Bert, and Cam to the president, and he invited them to visit him in the palace in Lima.

At Christmastime the visit to the palace became a reality. The three Anderson children and a number of their classmates were welcomed by a Navy officer who ushered them to the president's office. As they visited, Betsy presented a short speech in Spanish on behalf of the group, expressing their desire to serve as their parents were doing.

The president responded with words of appreciation for the help being extended to his people in the jungle, and he graciously received an Indian robe and bead necklace presented by one of the students. He then conducted a tour around the palace, leading them out into the central garden where hundreds of delicately designed blue tiles from Spain decorated the fountain area. Nearby was a fig tree reportedly planted by Pizarro, the Spanish conqueror of Peru. Photos by a palace photographer captured the exciting visit for future days.

During the Andersons' stay in the capital, the Ticunas at Cushillococha could not be forgotten. Letters from the tribe reminded them that Leonardo was taking care of spiritual needs and a medical worker was caring for physical needs. Lucas, son of a well-known witchdoctor, had trained in the Yarinacocha Clinic as well as in the Iquitos Hospital and he was now "Duturu" (Doctor) in his village. Lucas had also trained in the bilingual school, and he had committed his life to helping his people by means of modern medicine. The Ticunas' health was constantly improving!

Uiriu, the village carpenter, who now tells of how God changed his life.

Chapter Fourteen **TIMBER-R-R**

Early 1967 found the Andersons back home in the tribe with Lambert and Pachi beginning the translation of 1 John. As usual, there were interruptions.

One day they heard a loud voice in the direction of the lakefront: "Who is that one there on my lake? Don't you know that this lake belongs to me, and all the fish in it are mine?" It was Pablo's son Santos, obviously intoxicated, giving a speech with fitting gestures for the benefit of a passerby. Santos, one of the few remaining unbelievers, had long been known to the Andersons as "Santa Claus."

In their early days Lambert and Doris privately assigned nicknames so they could talk freely in English about people on the lake. There was "Crisco," "The Nose," "Charley Kite," "Charley Macaroni," "The Senator," "Freight Train," "Chopper," "Little John," and others. The Indians also had "play names"—"Alligator's Canoe," "Horse," "Little-Mouth Fish," "Nail," etc. These were in addition to their Spanish and clan names.

Pachi was open to explaining tribal practices whenever Lambert sought information.

The translation of 1 Timothy was well underway when Lambert received word that his father was near death. Taking a Peruvian Air Force plane making its weekly flight to Caballococha, he arrived in Iquitos and then got another plane the next day to Lima. Only after arriving in the United States did he learn that his father had died, but he arrived home four hours before the funeral.

During the month Lambert remained in Wisconsin,

Doris and the children continued the work in Cushillococha and then traveled to Yarinacocha in time for the beginning of school. Lambert returned and spent the remaining months of 1967 on language work at the base. One of the tasks was to write more songs.

By now Lambert and Pachi could carefully select Ticuna words whose tone patterns followed quite closely in the melody notes of several well-known Spanish songs. This furnished the Ticunas with some easier-to-learn songs.

At Christmas time Leonardo came to the base to take advanced studies, and a new milestone was marked when he consented to help Lambert with the translation project. They all returned to Cushillococha to dig deep into New Testament studies—and to observe a remarkable development around the village.

Before Lambert's first arrival, the Ticunas had made lumber by splitting logs with wedges and smoothing the outer sides, hewing them by hand until each half of the log became one fairly straight board. It took up to two days to make two boards. Later the Ticunas began to use a two-man hand saw about six feet long. Lambert helped by showing them how a log could be rolled onto a makeshift platform and then marked so a number of boards could be sawed from each log. Setting and managing the saw required skill, but two experienced men could saw up to twenty boards a day.

Though the rip-saw was an improvement over the hand-hewing method, it was limited in production and the men could work only with smaller logs. With the acquiring of their own land, the Indians owned considerable timber resources and they were concerned about using the logs felled while clearing the land.

"If we only had a small sawmill here, we could save our timber and have enough boards to build all our homes!" the Ticunas said to Lambert. At first the idea seemed wild. A sawmill would require specialized training and it would have to be a Ticuna-owned industry licensed by the government. But Lambert considered the suggestions seriously when he remembered an Indian reservation in northern Wisconsin which had its own sawmill. This had been a source of economic stability for the American Indians.

The first step toward the goal was the training of operators. Garcia Farias, a Ticuna in military service, was assigned to work in the army sawmill to learn all the operations. Ramiro, one of Pablo's sons, went to Tournavista, the R. G. LeTourneau settlement in the Peruvian jungle, to train in mechanics and engineering projects. There he learned engine maintenance, welding, and general repair in a three-year course.

Pancho Guerrero and Alberto Coello studied in the commerce course at Yarinacocha so they could do accounting as well as scaling of logs and lumber in Cushillococha. Four other young men were sent away to study carpentry, both furniture-making and the building of houses.

Other Ticunas entered additional specialties during these years of expansion: masonry, the care of cattle and chickens, and general agriculture. Angel, Leonardo's brother, studied electronics and learned radio repair at the Institute's radio lab. And Lucas Candido took the public health course at the Yarinacocha Clinic that qualified him to man the medical post in the tribe. Cushillococha was coming wide awake!

The engine for the mill was donated by a Wisconsin farming friend, Ben Sellen, who was interested in the Ticunas. The Corinth disc saw, bought in the United States, had been provided largely through various donations. To complete the purchase a loan was secured through World Neighbors, an organization dedicated to helping needy people to help themselves.

The Peruvian government expressed special interest in the Ticuna project, and when the sawmill equipment arrived in Pacallpa, the Peruvian Army offered to ship it on one of their boats free of charge to Iquitos, as they had helped with the light plant. Using another boat from there, they transported it downriver to the channel where it was transferred to smaller boats for carrying to the village. The chief of staff of the Army of the jungle accompanied the equipment all the way.

Lambert had contacted several men skilled in setting up sawmills, but none was available when the time came to install the machines. He and the Indians would have to do the work.

As they studied the blueprints it was evident that there were three basic requirements: the foundation would have to be solid, the machinery perfectly level, and the truck accurately aligned with the saw.

Gangs of Indians hewed out ironwood timbers a foot square and five feet long, while others leveled the ground. The hardwood base was laid and the sawmill platform was bolted into place. They built the track for the carriage and hung the saw. A slide was made to receive the logs from the lake and a log deck was erected to hold twelve to fifteen logs on the same level as the carriage for sawing. They even set up a small sawdust conveyer so no one would have to work in a pit. Instead, the conveyor could bring the sawdust to be dumped into handmade wheel barrows and wheeled off for disposal.

The big day came when the entire installation was completed and the saw-teeth bit into the first log, a Brazilnut tree that had been felled because it was growing on the site chosen for the sawmill. The Ticunas were launched on a new economic plane.

One person was lacking—a good administrator. Here again Leonardo stepped in to help. He had the admiration of his people and was capable in organization. Leonardo quickly noticed that the lumber was not put in classified stacks. He immediately stopped everything and had them classify all the lumber, stacking it according to species and size. He spent part of every day at the mill supervising the work and starting the men on efficient routines.

Very soon Cushillococha began to show the marks of the

sawmill. People began bringing in their logs to be sawed into boards for their homes. "Hey, where are you going with all those logs? What size of a house are you planning to build with all that timber?" they would josh one another, calling from the shore as industrious neighbors floated their logs to the mill. Half the lumber went to the logger and half to the sawmill to pay for maintenance and salaries.

In the midst of the hum and the sawdust, Lambert stood at the logging platform and lake and with watch in hand timed the Indians' production. A log was hoisted by winch to the platform and then rolled onto the carriage. From the moment the first cut was made by the disc saw until it was sawed into eighteen boards—thirteen feet long, ten inches wide, an inch thick—was exactly five minutes and twenty seconds! Cushillococha had entered the machine era!

In succeeding years, the government would contract for lumber to build new schools along the Amazon River frontier, assuring a good market for the Ticuna sawmill. The older Ticunas looking on could hardly believe the change from the days of subservience to outside managers.

"It's your land. Your country's chiefs want you to take good care of it." Lambert and José in front of village plaza marker. (Don Hesse)

Chapter Fifteen **"OURS"**

"We must concentrate on that which is basic—the salvation of souls through the Word of God in the tongues of the people." These words of Uncle Cam Townsend expressed the heartbeat of Lambert and Doris as they again immersed themselves in translation and literacy tasks. By late 1968 the book of Acts had been published and parts of its text incorporated into the reading program of the schools. Lambert wrote to U.S. friends: "The Ticunas are now eagerly reading the portions that they have in printed form, and through these Scriptures God is speaking in their own language to their hearts. As they learn more and more about him, we can see them growing in that childlike faith that carries them to heights that I couldn't dream would be possible."

The missionary life of Paul captured the imagination of the Ticunas. It so impressed Sixto and Anastacio, boys only ten and fifteen years old, that one afternoon around three o'clock they decided to leave their gardens and paddle upstream to preach to Ticunas in another village. Upon arrival they announced, "We would like to have a meeting—not wait until tonight, but right now!" The villagers gathered to listen to the boys tell what God was doing in Cushillococha. The people were enthusiastic and the boys reported the village urged them to come back and tell more.

Another time a half-dozen teen-agers, also readers of the book of Acts, piled into a canoe and paddled all through the day to get to Bellavista before sundown. That night they held a meeting to tell the people what God was doing for them. When a local witchdoctor opposed the visitors and refused to attend the meetings, one of the youths decided to fast and pray until the man responded. On the third night the witchdoctor came to the meeting and asked if he too might accept the Lord as his Savior.

Beginning in March, Leonardo was not only teacher and pastor, but also became Lambert's translation helper in every free moment. In some ways he seemed to have greater freedom than Pachi in expressing certain concepts in the Ticuna language. He was able to recognize spots where words should be less literal and somewhat rearranged to convey the thought more smoothly.

As they got into stride in translating, the books accelerated toward completion. 1 John, James, and 1 and 2 Timothy followed Mark and Acts. The fourth book of the New Testament, the Gospel of John, was next.

"This is the word that speaks to our hearts!" Leonardo exulted. "It is easy for us to read and easy for us to understand. It is ours—the Word of God to us!"

Leonardo spent a great deal of time reading the Scriptures by himself and meditating in addition to studying the New Testament during the translation hours. During these times God talked with him and led him to decisions of faith and purpose.

In September Lambert and Leonardo were back at the Yarinacocha base to follow a regular work schedule with nearby help. Looking at the seven New Testament books now completed, Lambert thought wistfully: "Someday the entire New Testament will be finished—perhaps even five years from now." There were twenty more to be done, including the most difficult such as Hebrews and Revelation.

That same month Uncle Cam arrived in Yarinacocha and he had lunch with the Andersons one day. Conversation was lively as Uncle Cam reported wonderful things happening in many countries among translators. Lambert and

Doris shared their exciting news about the Ticuna Scriptures completed and the impact of the Word of God upon the Ticunas at Cushillococha.

"They've constructed a new church building," said Doris, "but we wonder if they won't have to make it still larger. There are over two hundred children enrolled in the day school, and the adults have been attending evening classes so they can learn to read the Scriptures. Leonardo is such an unusual spiritual leader; he makes the Word of God live as he explains it in terms on the people's level. He's a pastor that any church would be proud to have. God has done such a special work in his heart that the believers trust his counsel implicitly."

Lambert added, "It's something like Jose told me the other day as we were chatting. 'Leonardo and his brother are two young men in which you can find no fault.' What a statement to make in an Indian community where all live close together and are so very observant. You know, Uncle Cam, God seems to be blessing the Ticunas far beyond anything that we thought could be possible. New people keep coming and there is an increasing rapport between the Ticunas of Cushillococha and the Spanish-speaking people of Caballococha. They really seem to respect one another now! Leonardo has done so much to build good relations. Recently when a land problem arose between the Indians and a patron who wanted to extend his pastures into their lands, someone suggested that they go to the police. Instead, Leonardo said, 'I know the man. Let me go and talk it over with him personally. I'm sure we can come to a peaceful solution.' As a result, the man agreed to recognize the Ticunas' rights and a potential conflict was avoided."

They told Uncle Cam how the Word was being taken to other areas. Cuere, despite his problems of 1965, was still active in traveling to other Ticuna villages upstream and downstream. He had brought back reports of strong interest in the gospel at homes he visited. In one place they had talked and sung practically all night, and Cuere could barely whisper the next day! In home after home he was asked to come back to tell more of this "Good Word."

There was so much to tell and the conversation never lagged, but suddenly it was time for Uncle Cam to hurry away to another appointment. Before leaving he said, "Let's have a word of prayer together." As they bowed, Uncle Cam prayed, "Lord, help Lambert and Doris to finish the translation of the New Testament before their next furlough in 1970."

As Uncle Cam walked out the door and down the path Lambert turned to Doris and said unbelievingly, "Did you hear what he prayed?"

"Yes," she almost gasped. "Before our next furlough would be two years!" An impossible idea! After the years of basic analysis, their translation work had just gotten a good start.

Lambert felt compelled to go directly to the translation desk where he began to do some figuring. First he counted the number of verses already done and he found they had translated approximately twenty percent of the New Testament. There was still eighty percent to go!

When Leonardo arrived for work that afternoon, Lambert told him what had happened. Uncle Cam's prayer was a challenge they must face. "What do you think, Leonardo?"

Lambert's direct question was unhesitatingly faced: "Well, if you are willing, I am." It was that simple. At that moment they determined before God that they would attempt the impossible with his help.

"No matter how long it may take us on a single verse," said Lambert, "we'll trust God to help us meet this goal to finish the first draft of the New Testament by furlough time in June of 1970." They had one year and nine months to achieve it!

"The actual style of the translation," George Cowan, president of Wycliffe, has said, "should be genuinely indigenous, that is, free from awkward or meaningless foreignisms." That remained their goal when translating a single verse sometimes took two hours as they sought for the central meaning of the verse and attempted to put it into words that sounded as if they had originally been spoken in Ticuna rather than Greek.

The Ticunas have no specific term for "sacred" or "holy," so the term *holy brethren* became *people who are good in God's sight.* The thought, *Draw nigh to the throne* must be written *Come to God our Chief,* since "throne" carries no significance in Ticuna.

Pushing against time, there didn't seem to be enough hours in a day. The team worked through the day on Saturdays and holidays and Lambert asked to be relieved of all other assignments. In the marathon exertion neither Lambert nor Leonardo was slowed down by illness.

One day Lambert noticed that they had translated forty verses in a single day. Incredible! Usually, especially when working in the epistles, they were happy to complete as many as ten verses a day. In the Gospels, where they encountered a great deal of narrative, they expected to go faster, and one day they translated sixty-five verses.

Doris had a significant part in the translation push. She typed up and checked the books being completed, and gave other aid as she could. "Doris," Lambert called one day, "we're really at a loss for this phrase: 'Their senseless minds were darkened.' " After a pause Doris thought of a possibility. "How about: 'Their minds became bad and they thought even more evil?' " Leonardo chimed in, "That's just the thought that came to me!"

Unity of thought was repeatedly sensed. Regarding "fishers of men," Leonardo observed: "You don't fish men, and if you say 'catchers of men' you may mean policemen!" The words were finally defined by saying, "Before, you worked at netting fish, but now you are going to work at my work and tell people my Word" (Matthew 4:19).

"Mysteries of the kingdom of God" was another thought-provoking phrase. Its simple equivalent became: "that word which at first only God knew."

The heart passage of the gospel, John 3:16, speaks in the

first person in Ticuna: "My Father God greatly loves the people of the world, and that is why, even though I am his only son, yet he sent (gave, turned over) me to the people in order that all who believe in me be not lost, but rather that they have life that never ends."

When Doris was not directly involved with the New Testament translation, she worked on literacy projects for the schools. Consulting with other linguists, she decided on what proved to be a major breakthrough for teaching Ticunas to read—the omission of tonal markings for most vowels. An experiment showed Ticunas could read more easily and yet follow the meaning of a sentence in the absence of the markings, therefore accent marks were added only where the context did not indicate which word was meant. As a result, printed Ticuna looked more like Spanish in its form, which proved to be a big step forward in the reading program.

Doris found Ticuna to be a rich language with much out-of-door material to draw on as she set up primers for the schools in Cushillococha and Bellavista. Some of the Indians also helped prepare reading materials. Pachi created many of the illustrations, and all of the text was checked by Ticuna teachers to make sure of its accuracy. The New Testament selections were readily accepted as a vital part of the literacy program.

Lambert and Leonardo left the hardest three books until the last. In Romans, Hebrews, and Revelation work slowed to only nine or ten verses on some days. A great deal of time was spent searching commentaries for help in interpretation of these books.

Romans 15:33 speaks of the "God of peace," an expression that has four possible meanings. It might be presented as "God who gives peace of heart"; the "God who causes peace between himself and man when he was at odds with men;" or ". . . when man was at odds with God"; or the "God who causes us to have peace among ourselves." After studying the context closely, Leonardo and Lambert decided to use "God who gives peace of heart."

The book of Hebrews was especially complex as much of the book assumes a previous knowledge of Jewish culture. A lot of time was spent going over the background of the book before the men felt they were ready to make meaningful translations.

A second problem was determining what to make explicit so readers would understand clearly and what not to make explicit because it would diverge from the central message while giving a detailed description of some unfamiliar item.

The phrase "sat down at the right hand . . ." holds no special meaning in Ticuna. Lambert decided to say: ". . . sat down next to his Father because he is now Chief of all." In several places it seemed best to describe the function of "high priest" as "the one who speaks to God on our behalf" rather than using the name.

During the intense days of racing with time, Leonardo and Lambert sometimes took a "breeze break" at the end of the afternoon. They would jump on a Honda cycle and go for a ride just to cool off. As Doris watched she would pray, "O Lord, there go those wonderful guys; don't let anything happen to them because I don't know how we'd ever get the translation finished." Week by week she watched their thrilling progress keep pace with the calendar.

The last book, Revelation, had several problems they hadn't encountered elsewhere. But the primary need was to accurately paraphrase meanings as they had been doing. "I am the Alpha and Omega" became, "Everything began with me, and nothing lasts longer than I." "You are lukewarm" was rendered: "You only believe a little bit, and only a little bit live for me." The metaphorical judgment depicted by "He will tread the winepress of the fury of the wrath of God" was streamlined into "He will greatly punish those people with that punishment which God in his anger has prepared."

June 10, 1970, was the red-letter date of completion—the last few verses of the last chapter of Revelation were written in Ticuna. Leonardo, Lambert, and Doris bowed their heads and gave thanks together for what God had done at the translator's desk. It had been the longest, most difficult period that Lambert could remember, but also the most rewarding. And they had an eighteen-inch stack of hand-written manuscripts, the first draft of the Ticuna New Testament, to present to the Institute office. Their work wasn't finished, but the Andersons' life goal seemed within reach!

Lambert contacted his mother by shortwave radio to give her the news that they had reached their goal only a week behind schedule. And when the Andersons reached the United States and talked by phone with Uncle Cam at Waxhaw, North Carolina, their first words informed him of another answered prayer!

Dried chambira palm fibers are twisted by hand to make strong cord for a native hammock. (Don Hesse)

Chapter Sixteen **HARVEST**

The familiar red and white postage stamp was a welcome sight as Lambert picked up the letter from the mailbox. "Less than ten days," he thought as he noted the postmark on the airmail envelope—Caballococha, Peru.

"Greetings from all of us in Cushillococha," wrote Leonardo. "We want you to know that we are following God well. And he has been doing a new work in our village. . . . There is a new unity among the believers, and God is showing us that he wants to perform miracles right here, today, just like he did for the first believers and apostles in the book of Acts. . . ."

All was well! Lambert thanked the Lord. The Ticunas didn't really need the Andersons; they needed God and he was demonstrating his presence through his Word and the ministry of his Spirit.

The first few months in the States had been filled with speaking engagements, finding a place to stay, purchasing a car for travel, and getting the children ready for school.

They had just gotten settled in Oshkosh, Wisconsin, when a call came from Wheaton College. One of the regular instructors in the foreign language department felt called to a ministry in Europe and the position was open to Lambert if he wanted it.

Lambert's first reaction was that Doris might not want to make a move now that they were finally settled in a home. Nor would his mother want them to move away during this precious furlough year. To his surprise, neither was opposed when he mentioned the possibility to them.

It would be a privilege to work with Dr. Bob DeVette, under whom they had studied. But it had to be God's will as well. As a fleece, Lambert asked God to arrange housing in Wheaton if this was what he wanted. College was due to start in ten days and all rented space would surely be occupied. But, twenty-four hours after going to Wheaton to check, housing was secured through a student who had just called the college about a house he was vacating.

In October another letter arrived from Caballococha, and this time Lambert's head drooped as he read Leonardo's words: "On September 5, the first Ticuna teacher, Pachi, went to be with the Lord."

How? What could have happened? The details followed. On a Saturday afternoon with no classes, Pachi had gone fishing with three children. A sudden storm descended and as Pachi guided his outboard canoe through the waves the tempest increased to such fury that the children huddled and hid their heads between their knees. Lightning and thunder filled the air.

The children suddenly realized the boat was going in circles. They looked back to see Pachi almost out of the canoe—only his foot hooked under the seat kept him from going overboard. They dragged him back into the boat —dead. Evidently lightning had hit him and traveled down his arm to the motor.

There were many signs that Pachi was prepared to meet his Maker. Leonidas, a teacher who was once a student of Pachi's, recalled a recent walk with Pachi and his remark: "You'll be here for a long time to come, but I won't be walking these paths much longer!"

Pachi had loved music. He could play beautiful melodies on both the violin and guitar, but his first love was his small accordion. The week preceding his death he had been practicing with students he planned to accompany in church. The songs were "Face to Face with Christ My Savior" and a Spanish song, "Cuando Cristo Venga" (When Christ Returns). On Sunday the students sang those two songs—at Pachi's funeral. They were songs of triumph for one who had joined the heavenly choir.

When Lambert talked with Bob Wacker about Pachi's death, the fellow missionary marveled: "What a wonderful picture that gave of what Jesus did for us! If Pachi had not borne that bolt of lightning it would probably have killed all the children in the boat. He took the full blow and the others were saved!"

The furlough year of teaching at Wheaton provided many gratifying experiences. Lambert enjoyed the fellowship with students who studied hard, played energetically, and found time to share their faith in ministries on and off campus. A big day came for the Andersons when Betsy, who had finished high school in January, was accepted at the college that now meant much more to them.

Letters kept coming from Cushillococha with news of God's blessings and Lambert and Doris looked forward to returning to Peru. God was proving to the Ticunas that his Word and power are just as real for Christians today as in New Testament times.

And it was evident that Leonardo, who had never spent a day in Bible School, was God's instrument for making himself real to the Indians. They all knew his way of life and listened hungrily to his teaching. Although extremely capable, he always presented himself as the "chief of sinners" in the manner of the Apostle Paul. Status and money were unimportant to Leonardo. Lambert remembered the time when Leonardo had taken special training in Iquitos and became eligible for a raise in salary. After several months Lambert asked him why he didn't fill out the formal request. Leonardo's reply was: "What do I need more money for? God has given me what I need to take care of my family. We have a house, food, and clothing. All I want is to serve the Lord, and he will take care of my needs."

What a joy to work with such a dedicated man!

Two weeks after their return to Peru, Lambert and Doris were back in Cushillococha. Leonardo's broad smile was their reward as he stood with other Ticunas on the bank to welcome them. Questions and answers came in a flurry as everyone talked at once and wanted to know how things had been going.

"You won't know this place," Leonardo declared. "God has been demonstrating his power to us, and practically all the people are following him. I know of only three families on the lake who aren't believers. And we never hear of a drunken party. We have a real unity among the believers —they consider one another brothers and sisters in the Lord and are really willing to help each other when there's a need. They're honestly obeying God and it's just like it says in the book of Acts: 'And the multitude of them that believed were of one heart and one mind.'

"God has also given us several new leaders from among the young people," Leonardo continued. "The wonderful part of it is that I didn't appoint them—God appointed them, and he's leading them to Bible School and to commit their lives to telling other Ticunas his message."

That night the bell rang and the Andersons joined the streams converging on the church. The light plant was temporarily out of fuel, so the Indians were using their kerosene lamps to light the church. The building had been lengthened and possessed a new board floor. There were dozens more benches than before, but they were filled and people stood along the walls. Children crowded the floor space around the small platform in front. Lambert and Doris found a seat toward the back as people shifted down the bench to make room for them.

An unfamiliar leader, evidently quite young and difficult to see because of the crowd and flickering lights, was at the platform directing the service. As he led the people through one song of praise after another, Doris finally leaned over to the woman next to her and asked who he was. "That's my son," the woman replied. She was Cuere's wife, and the leader was Beleno, the once-shy youth whom they remembered as being more-or-less a "nobody" around the village.

As their eyes became more accustomed to the dim lighting, they recognized several others for the first time. Barbina, a second wife of Uchu, a witchdoctor, was across the aisle singing along with everyone else. Lambert and Doris remembered seeing her many times sitting on her doorstep and laughing at the people passing on their way to church. Uchu was there, too, taking part just as intently.

Lambert was asked to come to the platform to give a report. He thanked God for taking care of the Ticunas while he was away and expressed his happiness at being back. "God has many people far away who have been praying for you" he informed them, "and now we see how he has answered their prayers. God is so good!"

The meeting lasted until almost ten o'clock when they sang a last song and a final prayer before leaving for their homes. Other villagers from both upstream and downstream shook the Andersons' hands at the door to welcome them back.

The next day several young men walked by the Andersons' house and Doris recognized them. She invited them in to visit and discovered they were the young men Leonardo had mentioned as the ones God had appointed to do his work. Calixto, Augusto, and Cecilio were Beleno's companions, and they each had a story to tell.

"I was so bashful that I hardly talked to my own mother," Beleno began. Lambert and Doris vaguely recollected his slouching figure going by a year or so before with a cigarette dangling from the corner of his mouth. He was trying to show he was important a year ago, he confessed. "But now I have accepted Jesus and I know what it's like to have his power in my life. I have a love that just runs over for everyone. When I received him into my heart it was such a joy that I can't explain it. I had a new love for my father and mother and I didn't get impatient with my brothers and sisters like before. There just aren't words to tell you what it's like." Tears glistened in his eyes.

"Now I want to go and tell everyone God's Word. I want them to know this new Friend who has done so much for me. Before, you would never have seen me up in front of the church, but God has taken away my shyness. There's so much happiness inside that I just have to tell it to others."

Cecilio suddenly turned and patted Augusto on the shoulder. "We're seeing miracles," he said, "just like when our brother Augusto came back to life."

"What?" she exclaimed, and the simple story unfolded.

They were all in church when Augusto suddenly fell forward off the bench. All efforts to revive him seemed futile. Nicasio, Leonardo's brother who is also a teacher, and others checked carefully for a heartbeat but there was none. An hour went by—he was obviously dead. His mother started wailing in sorrow, then someone said, "I believe God wants to do a miracle! Let's pray and ask him to make our brother alive again."

Hadn't God already healed Bataleon, Sebastian, and Manuel, all dying with a virus flu, and Miguel who had hemorrhaged all night, and Juan Farias who had suffered severe back pain for twenty years? Lucas' two small children, too, had been unable to eat for five days when their grandmother had the church elders pray and the children asked for food almost immediately. As the congregation prayed for Augusto, the young man's eyelids fluttered and then stayed open.

"All I can remember," added Augusto, "is that it was like being at the door of heaven. It was all so bright and beautiful I wanted to stay there all the time. Oh, it was so beautiful!"

The talk continued on late into the afternoon as the young men told how God had dealt with them as well as others of the village. The movement had started among the young people and spread to others.

Chichiria, a vivacious girl of eighteen, gave her life to Christ, as did her sister Elena. They told their father, Santos' older brother. In Chichiria's own words, "He was so furious we thought he would throw us out of the house. He didn't want to give up his old way of living. But we kept on praying and asking others to pray, and even though he got angry we still kept inviting him to church. One month later he finally agreed to go with us. He accepted Christ and now our whole family life is changed. My father and mother both love the Lord and we're so much happier now as a family."

The natural result was a desire to tell others. Beleno and Calixto traveled to villages along the huge Amazon island, Cacao, while Cecilio went to Bellavista. Two went to the village of Yanayaco, but they were confronted by machete-wielding drunks who vowed to kill them if they got out of their canoes. Their trips weren't always success-ful, but they were fulfilling God's command to go and tell others, even going to Spanish-speaking villages. Leonardo had counseled them always to go directly to the village authorities and ask permission before having services.

As the young Christians felt called to serve God, they started praying about where they should study. Remem-bering that Cuere, Beleno's father, had studied at the Swiss Indian Mission Bible Institute, they began to ask questions about it and ultimately filled out application blanks. Be-leno, Cecilio, and Sebastian—a young friend who wanted to study the Word— were accepted. They were joined later by Calixto and his new wife Elena, as well as Gerlardo and Eugenio, young Christian leaders from Bellavista. Chichiria enrolled in the Alliance Bible Institute in Huanuco.

While traveling through Yarinacocha, Beleno was asked to speak one Sunday evening to the members of the Insti-tute. Even though he was last on the program that night and the hour was late, he was repeatedly encouraged to con-tinue as he related what God had been doing. He closed his account by thanking everyone for their part in bringing God's Word in his own language—not only the Andersons but also the mechanics, the pilots, the radio technicians and operators, the doctors and nurses, and the teachers. "Thank you, *every one*," he emphasized.

Then he added a comment about the Ticunas' responsibility to tell their own people. "And," he concluded soberly, "maybe God has chosen us humble Indians to bring his Word to those who are so much more educated and wealthy."

The first Ticuna church, built in 1957. (Don Hesse)

Chapter Seventeen TICUNALAND

When a group of Ticunas from a small settlement upstream arrived at Leonardo's door to ask for help in getting a bilingual school started, he agreed to accompany them back to their village. Finding the community partly under water, Leonardo suggested they move to higher ground. The village leader suggested Bufeococha, a lake created centuries earlier by a switch in the Amazon's course.

Leonardo helped lay out the new village and then made arrangements with the ministry of education to establish a new school. He sent his brother, Nicasio, to be the teacher.

A delicate problem confronted the new teacher entering Bufeococha. The people had been following a cult of "the cross," a mixture of Christian ritual, Spanish choruses, and folk medicine. A large redwood cross stood in the middle of the village and the residents burned candles before it every sundown. When Nicasio arrived, their first question was, "Have you come to oppose our cross? If so, we're all leaving."

"No," he answered cautiously; "I have come to teach school."

"Well, then we'll stay," they responded.

The villagers were ready to begin school construction, and Nicasio joined in. Using knowledge and skills gained in Cushillococha, he made all the benches and tables for the students and a desk for himself. Since he had no house, he had to move his family into one end of the school when it was finished. He made no mention of his sacrifices in leaving a five-room house in Cushillococha built with sawed lumber and a corrugated aluminum roof. He was intent on serving the Lord in this isolated spot where the people resented any effort to present God's Word. "Lord, give us patience to stay and do what you've sent us here to do," Nicasio was to pray many times.

After two years of teaching and service, Nacasio was permitted to bring Beleno and Cecilio from Bible school to Bufeococha to hold preaching services. Night after night they spoke to a returning crowd, and twenty-five adults made decisions to follow Christ. The power of the cult was broken.

In Cushillococha people continued to be healed of illness through prayer. One day as Leonardo and Lambert talked in front of the Anderson's house, a young mother stepped up to Leonardo and said, "My child is very sick —could you come and pray for him?" Though his dinner was ready, Leonardo turned to his son Sixto and said, "Wait for me here, and I'll be right back." He followed the mother to her house where he prayed for the child and then returned to go home for dinner. Though nothing happened immediately, Lambert realized this was a part of Leonardo's ministry.

One day as Lambert walked home from church a newcomer named Abel stopped him and asked: "Mr. White Man, could you pray for someone who is sick?"

How could he say no? It was a new experience for Lambert, but he and Leonardo did pray to the same God!

"My mother-in-law is very ill and hasn't walked for a long time," explained the Indian. "Could you come to my house and pray for her?"

"Of course, I'd be happy to," Lambert agreed.

"When could you come? This afternoon, maybe?"

"I'll try. Let's see how things go."

But the afternoon went by and Lambert didn't find time to get to Abel's house at the far end of the village.

The next day Lambert went to work at the sawmill. He had barely started when Abel appeared with a smile on his face, and he stayed near all day helping Lambert, never mentioning his mother.

As darkness began to fall, Lambert said to Abel, "Let's go to your home." He knew why Abel had stayed around all day. On the way they met Leonardo and the three men continued on to Abel's house.

It was almost dark when they arrived. Abel and his wife took a small kerosene lamp into the back room used for sleeping, and then through the dark Lambert saw them half-drag, half-slide a pitiful looking creature across the floor. The woman was barely able to sit up amid much groaning. She was an emaciated pile of skin and bones. Evidently she had an advanced case of arthritis.

They propped her up in the doorway, and Lambert learned she hadn't walked for two years. Although it seemed a hopeless case, he suggested that they bow their heads, and laying his hand on the woman he prayed for God's help. Before leaving, he suggested that they put on hot packs and help her get some sunshine during the day which would at least make her more comfortable. He and Leonardo went home and the woman was more or less forgotten.

Two weeks later Lambert was sitting with Doris on the end of a bench in one of the middle rows at church, quietly waiting for the service to begin. Someone reached over and tapped him on the knee. He turned to see who wanted him—and almost fell off the bench. It was the lady whom he had prayed for!

"How did you get here?" was all he could breathe.

"I walked," was the reply.

He could hardly wait for church to finish so he could ask her what had happened. He certainly hadn't prayed with faith that she would walk again!

"After you prayed for me," she told him after the service, "I decided I'd at least try to walk. So I did, little by little, and today I thought I'd walk to church."

Lambert just shook his head, as he knew it was almost a

mile to her house. Finally he recovered enough to suggest that maybe she had been walking a little for some time. "No," she replied, "until you prayed I hadn't walked at all."

"But for how long? Several months?"

"Sir," Abel interjected, "we tell you. It has been two full years that she hasn't walked a single step."

Lambert's attempt to rationalize it all was futile. It was simply that the Indians believed and God had worked a miracle.

Other unusual things happened. While Doris was on a school supervision trip in Bellavista, she brought a new portable phonograph which had just arrived from Gospel Recordings. In the process of packing for the trip, she omitted the instructions for its operation and when she arrived she couldn't find the knob to wind it.

Eugenio, the young church leader, disappointedly carried it home to await the arrival of the knob the next time someone came from Cushillococha. The next day he appeared at the door of the Indian home where Doris was staying. "Sister, I found the knob," he announced. "The Lord showed me where it was. I dreamed last night that two of the teachers came and played the phonograph and I could hear the words and music in our language. I was feeling so bad because I couldn't play it, too, when all of a sudden a man in white in my dream said, 'You can play it if you look for the knob—it's there!' I could hardly wait for the sun to come up, and as it got a bit light outside I held the box over the wall and turned it over and over. All of a sudden that little spool-like thing moved and as I pushed it a little farther it dropped down and slid into position for winding. I turned it a few times and put on a record. It was beautiful! My family came out from under their mosquito nets to see what was going on, and I told them how God had told me that I could play it if I kept looking."

With the increased spiritual activities there was a new interest in reading. Adults were no longer content to be spoon fed by having children read to them. In 1972 Doris selected four capable young people and prepared them to take over classes. More than one hundred adults registered. Beginning groups finished three primers in six months. Others, a bit further along, finished three advanced primers and started Scripture reading.

For the adults the study meant leaving their gardens about 2 P.M. to get home in time to clean up and get to school by four o'clock, leaving older children to do baby-sitting. When classes were over, the women had to hurry home to get supper. By the end of 1973 there was a noticeable increase in the number of people participating in responsive reading in the church services.

A young man stood up in church to tell how different his life has been since he learned to read. "Get started in school!" he urged other adults. "Learn to read so you can study God's Word every day and know what he wants you to do!"

An academic boost came with the installation of a village library. Leonardo offered his school office to temporarily house three hundred books and pamphlets which had accumulated over the years from various sources. Two girls were placed in charge. Although the classifications included agriculture, sewing, cooking, literature, and history, Doris was pleased to note that a third of the thirty-plus books borrowed each day were from the religious section.

Sometime back Leonardo and Lambert had heard a graduation day message by don Victor Posadas at the Swiss Indian Mission. The next day Leonardo asked Lambert, "What impressed you most about the service yesterday?"

Lambert replied that there were a number of things that were impressive.

"No," Leonardo answered, "that isn't what I mean. What one part of the message really struck home to you?"

Lambert couldn't say that one part stood out above others to him.

"Well, the one point that really spoke to my heart,"

continued Leonardo, "was when don Victor said that if God calls us to serve him and we continue to turn him down, some day he won't call us any more and we'll be passed by. I don't want that to happen to me. My job, my house, everything I have, is secondary to God."

That dedication was deeper than words, and in 1973 Leonardo found a number of newcomers in the village. Among them was a young man from the Tacana River in Brazil. That night he told a story that Leonardo can't forget. "There are dozens of homes scattered all along the Tacana," he reported, "but no one has ever gone there to tell them God's Word. At first they were opposed to having anyone come. But now they would like to hear what God's message is. If you'd go, I know they'd listen to you."

Today Leonardo's heart is already out on the Tacana River and he has announced to the people of Cushillococha that there is no need for him to continue in their village when there are others who haven't heard the message of salvation.

One recent Sunday morning as the Ticunas worshiped together Calixto, the leader, announced, "This morning we'll be talking about what God has been doing for us, and we want to give an opportunity to all who desire to share their experiences with us."

Among the men who stood up was Teodoro, who had just come back from a week-long hunting trip. "One morning while we were deep in the jungle," he related, "my companion and I stopped a minute to look up at the sun bursting through a large opening in the trees and lighting the forest floor below. 'Isn't God wonderful' I cried out in exhilaration as I threw my arms out wide, turning to gesture at the beauty of God's creation above us. That instant my companion gave a startled cry and pointing to my foot, yelled, 'you're standing on a poisonous snake!' Unknown to me, my heel had come down on the head of the snake, crushing it as I turned to gesture.

"We continued on several hours more, and then stopped

to rest again. I found a felled log to stretch out on and lay back looking at the sky. As I started to let my arms fall down over the sides of the log, I glanced over to one side. Right there was a snake curled up, already stiffening itself to strike my hand which I snatched back. The Lord really watches over us, doesn't he?"

Another one who shared was Meduchu, a man of about thirty who lost his mother when he was a small boy, and then his father was killed by a machete-armed Indian, taking revenge for supposed witchcraft. Meduchu began, "Last year in my home I had a real problem which I finally got straightened out when our brother Leonardo prayed and fasted with us one Sunday. It had begun after I turned my life over to God about three years ago. I couldn't read very well then, but as I have attended adult school these last two years, I have been reading the Word more and more. I didn't want to leave it even to go out to my garden and work. But my wife wasn't in accord with me at first, and I wept with sadness as she belittled God's Word. She was only thinking about working in the garden to get money to buy new clothes, while I wanted to keep on reading the Word. But now God has worked in her heart too, and we're so happy—united in the Word, and she wants to listen when I read it.

"Remember how I used to be the first one at the fiestas to play my harmonica for everyone to dance? And I laughed at God's Word. But life is so different now. Living for the Lord is so satisfying."

A third testimony was that of Uilian, a young Ticuna carpenter who wanted to share a story that had been on his heart for a long time. "I was working downstream in Leticia about three years ago," he explained, "when one night I had a dream. I saw an extremely bright light shining down from the sky onto the church at Cushillococha. The whole surrounding area was lit up with the brightness, and there in the center stood our brother Leonardo, holding out God's Word to the crowds of people gathered. And over on the side I saw several young people holding out the Word also. I was so gripped by the dream that I left at dawn, paddling twelve hours upstream.

"My mother met me with the words, 'Everything is changed here. We'll be meeting tonight and then you'll see what I mean.'

"As the bell rang and the people began to gather I couldn't believe my eyes—there were so many people, five or six hundred, all packed in and standing around as the service began. Kerosene lamps made flickering shadows along the walls and I strained to recognize the young person who had just stood up in front—yes, it was one of those I had seen in my dream. The speaker was telling about the deep joy within him since he had given himself completely to God's will.

"I had grown up hearing God's Word, but had never made a personal commitment to the Lord Jesus Christ. Since then, I have had a real change. It's been a new life since I really gave my heart to him." And gesturing toward himself, he concluded, "This isn't the same man you used to know. Now I love to read the Word and it penetrates into every area of my life."

Today God speaks to the Ticunas, and as they hear him a unique church is being built—not a structure erected but a fellowship of new people built by God's Holy Spirit. Faithful supporters prayed and gave their money to bring the gospel to Ticunaland, but God gave the spiritual increase which will multiply forever.

Looking back over twenty-one years in Ticunaland, the Andersons are filled with the deep joy of those who follow the will of God. "We have reached only one of the two thousand tribes awaiting God's Word," they say. "But as God calls others and they take God's message to more tribes, the goal of reaching every people in their own language will be accomplished in this generation."

God's work among the Ticunas is not finished either spiritually or socially but this "city of God" in the jungle now lives in the Light that can brighten the whole world. "Happy is that people whose God is the Lord" (Psalm 144:15).

Uncle Cam Townsend and guests who arrived from Lima and Iquitos for the inauguration of the light plant. (Eugene Loos)

Epilogue

WILLIAM CAMERON TOWNSEND
Founder of the Wycliffe Bible Translators

With God's Word in their own tongue and the Holy Spirit working so powerfully, the Ticunas will not need the Andersons much longer, and Lambert and Doris can move on to another language group. Why should missionaries stay on indefinitely?

Wycliffe Bible Translators believe in pioneering. They feel that once a people have God's message of love in their own tongue, and some at least have learned to read it and take it as the rule of life, they can conduct their own affairs under the guidance of the Holy Spirit. The translators can go on to a new situation where darkness reigns as it once did in Cushillococha. They can learn another language and translate the Word into it. Why should one Cushillococha be enough for the Andersons?

Two young women who joined the Wycliffe Bible Translators in the '40s have now translated the New Testament into three Indian tongues. However, even if many of the 600 teams of translators presently in W.B.T. do a second or third translation, we still urgently need several thousand more translators and support personnel to insure the completion of the task in this century. Since more languages are being discovered, there are still 2,000 tongues to go!

Who will volunteer and thus be instrumental in bringing the light of the Word to those overlooked corners of the earth?